TRAUMA TREATMENT TOOLBOX FOR TEENS

144 Trauma-Informed Worksheets and Exercises
to Promote Resilience, Growth & Healing

Kristina Hallett, PhD, ABPP · **Jill Donelan**, PsyD

Editing: Jenessa Jackson, PhD
Layout: Bookmasters & Amy Rubenzer
Cover: Amy Rubenzer
ISBN: 9781683732136

PESI Publishing & Media
pesipublishing.com

ABOUT THE AUTHORS

Kristina Hallett, PhD, ABPP, is a board-certified clinical psychologist, executive coach, keynote speaker and associate professor of psychology at Bay Path University. She is a Fellow of the American Academy of Clinical Psychology. Dr. Hallett is the author of the international best-sellers *Own Best Friend: Eight Steps to a Life of Purpose, Passion, and Ease* and *Be Awesome: Banish Burnout, Create Motivation from the Inside Out.*

Dr. Hallett has based her career in public service, working with disadvantaged youth in the community, as the Director of two outpatient clinics, the Director of Children's Services for a behavioral health system, Director of Psychological Services in the Connecticut prison system, and as the Director of Clinical Training for a pre-doctoral internship program for a community mental health center. She specializes in working with teenagers, complex trauma and dissociative disorders, anxiety, depression and personality disorders.

Jill Donelan, PsyD, is a licensed clinical psychologist specializing in the treatment of children, adolescents, and families. She is Assistant Professor of Psychiatry at University of Massachusetts Medical School at Baystate, clinical supervisor for the Child Partial Hospitalization Program at Baystate Children's Hospital in MA, and adjunct professor in graduate psychology at Bay Path University.

She has over a decade of experience in providing treatment to youth, with specialties in the treatment of trauma and severe mental illness. Dr. Donelan also has a wealth of experience in supervision and program development and evaluation. She works with interdisciplinary teams to implement evidence-based, culturally sensitive clinical practices. Dr. Donelan has dedicated her career to meeting the needs of underserved and vulnerable communities.

Dr. Donelan earned her doctorate in clinical psychology from Baylor University in Waco, TX. She previously served as the Director of Psychology and Internship Training at The Village, Inc. in Hartford, CT.

TABLE OF CONTENTS

INTRODUCTION

This workbook is intended to be a toolbox for clinicians working with teenagers who have experienced trauma. It can be considered a supplement that adds to clinicians' existing skills and expertise. For clinicians who have little experience working with teenagers, this workbook helps break down treatment skills that can, at times, be challenging to present to the adolescent patient. In particular, we help translate these skills in a manner that is more developmentally appropriate for the teenage audience. At the same time, clinicians who are highly experienced in working with adolescents will also find this workbook to be of use, as it presents a variety of practical ways to reinforce skills with adolescents. Given that novelty is of importance when working with adolescents, having a variety of ways to present information increases the likelihood of therapeutic success.

In writing this workbook, we drew from interventions and treatment approaches that spanned a wide variety of theoretical models, including cognitive behavioral therapy (CBT), dialectical behavior therapy for adolescents, play therapy, acceptance and commitment therapy, mindfulness, solution-focused therapy, and trauma-informed cognitive behavior therapy. We also relied on the most recent publications and research from the Substance Abuse and Mental Health Services Administration (SAMHSA) for relevant definitions regarding trauma and trauma-informed care.

In doing so, we decided to base this workbook on a **trauma-informed approach**, which is different from specific forms of trauma treatment (which are beyond the scope of this workbook). According to SAMHSA (2012), a trauma-informed approach involves four Rs: "(1) *realizing* the prevalence of trauma; (2) *recognizing* how trauma affects all individuals involved with the program, organization, or system, including its own workforce; (3) *responding* by putting this knowledge into practice; and (4) *resisting* re-traumatization." A trauma-informed approach is particularly relevant because many teens who have experienced trauma will not necessarily present with classic symptoms of post-traumatic stress disorder (PTSD) symptoms. Rather, they may present with symptoms such as anxiety, depression, anger, social difficulties, academic problems, and family conflict. While their symptoms, and often their diagnosis, are not trauma-specific, careful investigation of their life history reveals the many and complex ways in which their experiences of trauma contribute to their current struggles. Therefore, a trauma-informed approach to treatment provides a framework for not only addressing their primary symptoms, but also for understanding and acknowledging the ways in which these symptoms have formed as a result of stressful life experiences.

TRAUMA IN TEENAGERS

"Individual trauma results from an event, series of events, or set of circumstances that is experienced by an individual as physically or emotionally harmful or life threatening and that has lasting adverse effects on the individual's functioning and mental, physical, social, emotional, or spiritual well-being" (SAMHSA, 2014). **The key point in understanding trauma is not the exposure to a stressful event in and of itself, but rather the individual's experience of that event. A stressful event becomes traumatic when the demands of the situation overwhelm the individual's ability to cope with the situation.** Individual responses to traumatic experiences are modulated by many factors, including genetic and biological factors, the context of family and other support systems, and individual vulnerabilities related to previous life experiences. In this way, two teens may experience the exact same stressful event, a natural disaster for example, and have two completely different outcomes. Whereas one teen may experience fear and distress during the event and quickly return to his or her baseline functioning once the event is over, another adolescent may develop intense anxiety, fear, and anger in the aftermath of the same event. It is also true that a teen may not be aware of how traumatic an experience was until some later date. In addition, the teen may not realize how the traumatic experience feeds into later problematic or self-harmful attitudes and behaviors.

While it is not the intent of this workbook to provide specific treatment approaches for individual types of trauma that may be experienced by adolescents, it is relevant to note that adolescents may experience any number of types of trauma in their lifetime. While the teen themselves may tend to think of "trauma" as physical or sexual abuse only, the reality is that there are many other types of stressful life experiences that can result in trauma. This becomes more complicated when you consider that many teens in treatment have experienced multiple types of trauma over their lifetime, and their response to each traumatic event is at least in part influenced by their previous trauma history. Often, a teenager will be referred to treatment due to one specific trauma, and only through careful history taking are multiple earlier traumatic events identified. Therefore, in evaluating teens, clinicians should keep in mind a broad spectrum of potentially traumatic life experiences, including:

- Abuse (emotional, physical, sexual)
- Community violence
- Complex trauma
- Domestic violence
- Early childhood trauma
- Medical trauma

- Natural disasters
- Neglect
- Refugee trauma
- School violence
- Terrorism
- Traumatic grief

WHY IS THIS WORKBOOK GEARED TOWARD TEENS?

Unfortunately, traumatic experiences are not rare in adolescence. The National Survey of Children's Exposure to Violence (Finkelhor, Turner, Hamby, & Ormrod, 2011) found that almost half of adolescents between the ages of 14 and 17 had experienced some form of victimization in their lifetime, including instances of physical assault, bullying, sexual victimization, and abuse or neglect. Similarly, the 2015 National Crime Victims Week Resource Guide found high rates of assault, property victimization, childhood maltreatment, and sexual assault in this same age group (OVC, 2015). The long-term implications of trauma during childhood and adolescence are significant and well-documented. A groundbreaking study of Adverse Childhood Experiences (ACEs) demonstrated the cumulative power of stressful life events in predicting negative health and well-being outcomes later in life. Specifically, as the experience of ACEs increased, so did the risk for:

- Heart and vascular diseases
- Alcohol, nicotine, and drug use
- Adolescent pregnancy
- Depression and suicide attempts
- Poor academic achievement

- Financial stress
- Fetal death
- Sexual violence
- Losses in health-related quality of life

Although there are a variety of treatment approaches that are commonly used with *both* children and adolescents in the treatment of trauma, there are clear developmental differences between young children and older teenagers, and successful treatment thus requires that appropriate developmental modifications be made. Although one particular treatment modality – trauma-focused CBT – has been shown to have significant efficacy in working with children who have experienced childhood maltreatment (Cohen, Mannarino, & Deblinger, 2006), it can still pose some barriers when working with older adolescents. In particular, trauma-focused CBT relies upon significant involvement of parents and families, which can be difficult to balance in conjunction with teenagers' developmental desire for independence, autonomy, and privacy. Moreover, adolescents who have experienced trauma are prone to engaging in avoidant behaviors, such as substance use, and they often are minimally motivated to participate in therapy. Given the relative lack of effective treatment approaches that are specifically geared toward teenagers 14 years and older (Matulis, Resick, Rosner, & Steil, 2013), we sought to write this book in order to provide clinicians with developmentally appropriate tools that increase teenagers' likelihood of treatment engagement and provide a means of focused skill-building.

Given that many clinicians struggle in connecting with adolescents – and that adolescence is a time of ever-changing attitudes, perspectives, and behaviors – using guidelines such as those recommended by both SAMHSA and the National Child Traumatic Stress Network (NCTSN) increases the likelihood that clinicians will be able form a positive therapeutic relationship with their teenage client. This workbook (and our own therapeutic relationships) are based on the guidelines and principles mentioned above.

The excitement, and the challenge, of working with teenagers is in finding ways to connect and relate. Many times, adolescents are reluctant, or lack the skills, to engage in insight-oriented therapeutic communication. The worksheets provided in this book seek to address these issues by providing exercises that are geared to start or increase conversation between the clinician and the adolescent, help teens to understand the multiple factors that may be influencing their behaviors and beliefs, and provide teens with skills to manage their emotions and symptoms in a healthy manner that promotes resilience and growth.

DEALING WITH TRAUMA
Handout for Teens

• • • • • •

Sometimes, life is really hard. Sometimes it's really hard for a LONG time. But there's good news. Thanks to what we've learned from research in the areas of neuroscience and psychology – as well as the experience of many people – it's possible to feel better. Even if that doesn't seem at all possible today, it really is.

This workbook was developed for people just like you: Teenagers who have dealt with difficult, challenging, and truly crappy circumstances. Teenagers who struggle with figuring out how to feel better when it just doesn't seem possible. Teens who sometimes make choices that don't really help, but seem like the best possible idea in that moment. Teens who aren't sure how to connect with other people, and who experience worry, anxiety, anger, and sadness. Teens who want to develop a life that feels worth living but don't know what to do.

The Oxford English Dictionary defines trauma as a "deeply distressing or disturbing experience." That covers a lot of ground. Trauma can be something you personally experienced, witnessed, or that happened to someone you know. Trauma can include the bombing of the Twin Towers in New York City, school shootings, Hurricane Katrina, and the wildfires in California. Trauma can be the death of a relative, the divorce of your parents, or moving to a new school. Seeing your parents fight or experiencing any kind of domestic violence is trauma. Trauma can also be something physical, mental, or emotional that happens to you. Being the victim of bullying (either in person or on the internet) is a form of trauma. In fact, if we listed all of the different kinds of trauma, this workbook would be way longer than it is already!

Trauma takes many forms

Here's the thing: No two people will respond to the same situation in the same way; that's just a part of how we are unique. What may be traumatic for one person may be just temporarily stressful to another.

If you have experienced some form of trauma, then the good news is that there are ways to move into recovery and feel better. Maybe you think that what you've experienced is "not that bad." Or maybe it seems unbearably awful. Either way, the exercises in this workbook are designed to help you to discover and use new (or improved) ways of coping.

It's also important for you to know that this workbook includes a series of exercises and worksheets that are helpful to anyone, whether or not they have experienced trauma. This workbook is all about skill-building, and we can all benefit from increasing the number of skills in our toolbox. Each chapter has suggestions to help you live your best life and that increase your knowledge, awareness, and ability to deal with whatever comes up. You know – real life.

There are chapters on identifying and understanding emotions (because there really are more emotions than mad and sad), and chapters that teach you about the ways in which stress impacts your body and your brain. There are also chapters that teach you how to breathe (yeah, you know one way to breathe, but you'll learn a few other ways that are guaranteed to make a difference in dealing with anxiety or overwhelming feelings!). There are also chapters that focus on values and goal setting, because this workbook is not just about dealing with today. It's also a tool to put your future into motion.

Building the skills taught in this workbook will help you become more resilient and will decrease the likelihood that future situations will result in traumatic symptoms. You can think of trauma like rising water. People start out at different heights – which reflects their innate resources/resiliencies – but they can add to their "height" by using the building blocks of skills that are in this workbook.

How to Use This Book

You can go through the workbook from beginning to end, or you can skip around, starting wherever makes sense. Some people like to do the "easy" stuff first, and that's absolutely unique to each individual, since what is considered "easy" is different for everyone. Other people start with whatever seems most useful in that moment. Bottom line: There is no wrong way to use this workbook, and there is no way to do it wrong, because simply putting forth the effort to learn and try new things is success!

EMOTION SKILLS

Individuals who have experienced trauma, whether one-time traumatic events or ongoing traumatic stressors, often present with symptoms related to negative changes in thought or mood. They may experience emotional numbing or detachment, a decrease in their ability to experience positive emotions, and an increase in irritability or anger (American Psychiatric Association, 2013).

Given that trauma and post-traumatic adversities can strongly impact child development (NCTSN, 2012), it is not uncommon to find that teens who have experienced trauma have a somewhat limited emotional vocabulary and often struggle to appropriately express their emotions across varying situations. For example, teens may be more comfortable expressing aggravation and anger, when underlying emotions of fear and anxiety are really the core issue. They also frequently exhibit substantial guardedness that is expressed through either an "I don't care" or an "I'm fine" attitude. It can be tempting to understand this as part of the general reluctance often seen in teenagers regarding talking to adults, but we suggest maintaining an open awareness that perceived resistance may be a function of previous trauma exposure. Keep in mind that teens don't necessarily view their experiences as traumatic, especially if they have no alternate experiences as a model.

For example, imagine a 16-year-old female who is sent to therapy with a history of self-harm behavior. As she relates her history, she discloses her first sexual experience was at 14 years old, when she paid a visit to a 32-year-old army veteran who had been threatening her mother. She agreed to have sex with him so that he would leave her mother alone. However, when asked about a history of trauma, she denied experiencing any physical, sexual, or emotional abuse. She didn't view any of this experience as a trauma because she was acting in a way to help her mother and felt that she was "in control" of the situation. She had no awareness of the manipulation, coercion, or inappropriateness of the experience. She also had no language to express the depths of despair, self-hate, disgust, and shame she felt for engaging in this behavior.

Accordingly, one focus of treatment involves teaching teenagers to expand and vary their vocabulary, so they can express many different feeling states, both positive and negative. Indeed, understanding and expressing emotions is a fundamental skill in the treatment of trauma for people of all ages. Broadening the range of identifiable emotions helps teens create a bigger canvas from which to understand their life and experiences. Supporting teens in expanding the knowledge and range of positive emotions in particular can also be a major factor in developing resilience and building hope. Once teenagers develop the ability to identify and express their emotions, this can serve as a building block for more complex skills, such as emotion regulation and assertive communication.

In addition to developing and expanding the adolescent's vocabulary for expressing emotions, it is important that teenagers develop the ability to relate these concepts back to their personal experiences. Given that trauma often impacts self-perception and frequently leads to avoidance, it is not uncommon to find that even when teenagers have a sufficient vocabulary regarding their feelings, they still struggle to apply this knowledge to their own lives. For example, they may be unable to label any of their *own* feelings, unable to label more complex emotions (e.g., disappointed versus sad), or able to only identify with a narrow range of feelings (e.g., only mad, irritated, and angry). Through the development of basic emotion skills, teenagers are given the language they need in order to describe their internal world and experience. Being able to tune into their own experience is a critical first step in their eventual capacity to understand the impact of trauma on their life, which is known in the trauma treatment literature as "integration" or "making meaning" (Spinazzola, 2010). In considering the previous case example, the teen first needed to develop a broader range of emotional language, then an awareness of how power differential and a history of parentified behavior impacted her decision-making. Through an exploration of safety, relationships, and boundaries, treatment centered on how issues of loyalty and core beliefs ("Do anything for your family and don't share information with any outsiders") shaped her limited ability to trust, as well as her tendency to take on personal responsibility for others without care for herself.

When taught during the early phases of treatment, emotional awareness and expression can facilitate the development of a trusting, collaborative, and respectful therapeutic alliance. In the adolescent stage of development, many teenagers are unwilling participants in treatment, and they are often compelled to attend by parents, caregivers, or other authority figures (e.g., schools, courts system). Even adolescents who choose to participate in therapy often feel that their own experience is unique and cannot possibly be understood by someone else. **Each time the adolescent expresses their experience of a situation and how they feel about it, the therapist has the opportunity to build rapport by helping the teen feel seen, understood, and accepted, regardless of whether they view themselves as a voluntary participant in treatment.**

In addition, the development of basic emotion skills will help the adolescent and therapist communicate more effectively about any emotional reactions that the teen has in session, as well as any emotional changes that occur over the course of treatment. Being able to maintain open lines of communication is particularly important in the treatment of adolescents, as their opinion of their progress in treatment may vary greatly from that of their parents or guardian. By giving teenagers the language to express their own experience of treatment, the therapist can also encourage them to express their own age-appropriate preferences within therapy. Additionally, the adolescent's self-reported progress over the course of treatment can provide useful information for important stakeholders, such as parents, guardians, insurance companies, or the court system.

Finally, the development of basic emotion skills can also be particularly useful to families of teenagers, whether or not these family members themselves have experienced trauma. Both teens and their caregivers can benefit from improved communication, increased understanding, and – ultimately – stronger connection when they are able to apply basic emotion skills to the more complex situations that arise in parent-teen relationships.

HOW TO INCORPORATE THE EMOTION SKILLS WORKSHEETS

The worksheets in this section cover basic emotion skills, including labeling and expressing emotions, as well as applying the vocabulary of emotions to personal experiences. When teaching adolescents how to label their feelings, it is important to be sure to cover the full breadth of emotions. Doing so may initially pose challenges for those teens whose trauma has resulted in a restricted range of affect. In these cases, using examples from movies, books, or their peers may be necessary to assist the adolescent in recognizing the full range of feeling states.

The activities provided here include the core emotions of happy, sad, scared, mad, surprised, and disgusted – and they also include space for other emotions to be added in. The therapist should invite teens to include any emotions that are of particular significance to them, including any problematic emotions, emotions that they would like to experience more frequently, or emotions that they may have difficulty identifying or expressing. In this manner, each activity can be tailored to meet the unique needs of the individual.

When working with teenagers regarding the expression of emotions, it is important to note that people typically think of expressing emotions in the verbal sense (e.g., having the words to speak, write, or otherwise label specific feeling states). However, this is only one way for feelings to be expressed. Given that feelings are activated and processed in parts of the brain that are distinct from the language center of the brain, being able to express feelings in non-verbal ways is also critically important. Therefore, several worksheets include creative prompts and ideas about how teens can express a range of feelings using art, music, and even physical movement. Artistic or creativity ability is not required, and even those teens who are worried about their creative skills can benefit from completing these activities. Because these non-verbal methods allow the adolescent to access and express their emotions in a different manner, it is the *process* of completing the activity that is therapeutic, not the final product.

This section also pays special attention to anxiety, given that an increase in anxious feelings is an almost universal response to trauma. Anxiety can manifest in many ways among adolescents, and a fundamental goal of this section is to normalize this response to traumatic events. The activities assist adolescents in recognizing that their anxiety is an understandable response to challenging or traumatic situations, and it gives them a framework for understanding different types of anxiety that they may be experiencing. Finally, adolescents are guided through activities that focus on social anxiety. Because adolescence is a developmental period when social relationships take on increased significance, even teenagers who do not exhibit "clinically significant" social anxiety can benefit from developing a greater understanding of how anxiety impacts their interactions and relationships with peers.

FEELINGS VOCABULARY

· · · · · ·

Identify as many words as you can for different types of feelings. For now, it is not important if these feelings apply to you or whether they match how you currently feel. You just want to list as many feeling words as you can think of.

Set a timer for 3 minutes and write down as many feeling words as you can in the following space. Don't worry about spelling or being "right." Use whatever words or phrases come to mind that could be used to describe different feelings. Stop when the timer goes off.

CATEGORIES OF FEELINGS

• • • • • •

Using the list of words and phrases you came up with in the "Feelings Vocabulary" activity, sort your list of feelings into general categories in the following chart. If you have words that do not fit into these categories, feel free to use extra paper to create your own categories. Just make sure that you have at least 3 or 4 words in each category. You can use a thesaurus or ask for help if you are stuck.

Happy:	Sad:
Mad:	**Scared:**
Disgusted:	**Surprised:**
Other:	

FEELINGS INTENSITY

. . . . . .

Feelings can be experienced to varying degrees or intensities. For example, happy feelings may be experienced as "content" (low intensity), "cheerful" (medium intensity), or "ecstatic" (high intensity).

Using the words you came up with in the "Feelings Vocabulary" and "Categories of Feelings" activities, categorize your feelings words into low, medium, and high intensity using the following chart. Try to fill each square with at least two different words. You may use a thesaurus, the internet, or the help of your therapist or a friend/family member to help with any areas where you might get stuck.

Keep this chart as a handy reminder of all the ways you can describe or express different emotions, and add new words and phrases to your list when you hear or think of them. You can also refer back to this list when you are struggling to label or express the way that you are feeling in a particular situation.

Low intensity	Medium Intensity	High Intensity
Happy		
Mad		

Low intensity	Medium Intensity	High Intensity
Scared		
Surprised		
Disgusted		
Other: _____		

FEELINGS THERMOMETER

· · · · · ·

A feelings thermometer is one way to measure how intense a certain feeling is at any given time. Select one feeling (happy, mad, sad, scared, surprised, disgusted, or another) to use for the following thermometer.

Once you have selected the feeling, see if you can think of words that describe how that feeling feels at 25, 50, 75, and 100% intensity. For example, if your feeling is happy, 25% might be "Just okay," 50% might be "Good," 75% might be "Excited," and 100% could be "Overjoyed." For each of these intensities, please note how you notice this feeling in your body. For example, when you feel excited, you may feel your heart rate increase, and you may notice energy in your arms and legs.

Once you have filled in your thermometer, you can use it at any time to assess how you are feeling.

— 100%

Feeling: _____

At 100% I feel: _____

— 75%

My body cues are: _____

— 50%

At 75% I feel: _____

My body cues are: _____

— 25%

At 50% I feel: _____

My body cues are: _____

At 25% I feel: _____

My body cues are: _____

TRACKING FEELINGS OVER TIME

· · · · · ·

Sometimes, we forget that how we feel in the moment is not the way that we feel every day, all day. Tracking your feelings over time is one way to see your feelings more objectively, to monitor how you are improving over time, and to share your feelings with others (like a therapist or parent).

When tracking your feelings, you may want to monitor your feelings from day to day, or you may want to look at how your feelings vary throughout the course of a single day. As you track your feelings, you may become more aware of how your feelings change from moment to moment and from day to day, and you may also notice the situations that cause certain feelings to be more or less intense.

Use the charts on the next page to track your feelings over the course of a single day or one week.

1. Select one feeling that you want to track over time. It may be a feeling that has been troubling you (anxiety or sadness) or a feeling that you would like to experience more often (happiness or peacefulness).

2. Decide if you will be monitoring that feeling over the course of a day **or** over a week, and then pick the corresponding chart that follows.

3. Using a scale of 1 to 10, mark the intensity of that feeling on an hourly or daily basis (1 = lowest possible intensity of that feeling and 10 = highest possible intensity).

4. If you are using the weekly chart, then for each day rate how intense the feeling you are tracking was on that day. You may only have experienced the feeling for a brief time, or it may have been a feeling that was present most of the day. Pick a number between 1-10 that captures how intense the feeling was on that day.

5. At the end of the day or week, look back at your chart, and respond to the questions on pages 11 & 12.

Feeling I will track this week: _____

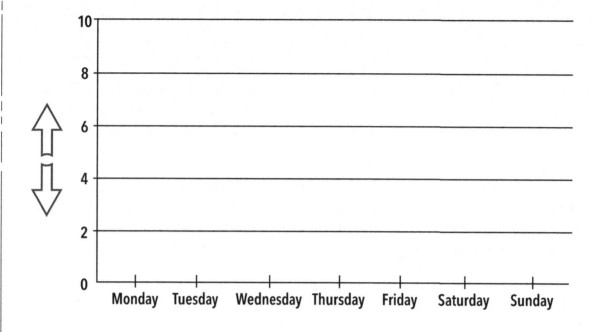

10

8

6

4

2

0

Monday Tuesday Wednesday Thursday Friday Saturday Sunday

Feeling I will track today: _____

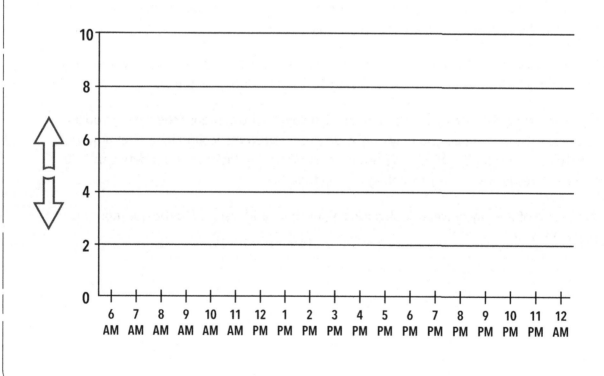

10

8

6

4

2

0

6 AM 7 AM 8 AM 9 AM 10 AM 11 AM 12 PM 1 PM 2 PM 3 PM 4 PM 5 PM 6 PM 7 PM 8 PM 9 PM 10 PM 11 PM 12 AM

OBSERVING MY FEELINGS

· · · · · ·

1. Look at your daily or weekly feelings record. Start just by observing and sticking to the facts. What do you notice about your feelings from your chart? Does anything pop out at you? Do you notice any patterns or trends? Is there anything that surprises you?

_____

_____

_____

_____

_____

_____

2. Now, consider what you might learn from your feelings chart. What does the chart tell you? What does the chart NOT tell you? What possible explanations might there be for the patterns or trends in your chart?

_____

_____

_____

_____

_____

_____

3. Time to celebrate! What is the "good news" in your chart? What are the successes or high points?

_____

_____

_____

_____

_____

4. Finally, it's time to think about next steps. Is there other information you need in order to understand your feelings better? What changes would you like to see in your feelings? What might you learn from tracking your feelings that could help you to make these changes? *Don't worry if this part seems hard or overwhelming. As you work through the exercises in this workbook, you will learn many strategies that can impact your feelings. For now, it is perfectly fine to just be more aware of how you feel.*

_____

_____

_____

_____

_____

FEELINGS IN MY BODY

· · · · · ·

Sometimes, we don't realize that we feel certain emotions at specific places in our body. For example, many people feel fear in their belly or in their throat. Some people feel happy in their heart, and other people feel happy in their belly. You can even feel happy in your toes! It's unique to everyone, so there's no right or wrong place to feel your feelings.

It helps to learn the "language" of our bodies because our bodies can give us clues to how we are feeling when we are stuck, uncertain, or can't seem to untangle a bunch of different feelings. This exercise will help you to start to decode the language of feelings in your body.

Using the outlines on the next page, indicate where in your body you feel each of the following feelings:

- Happy
- Sad
- Mad
- Scared
- Surprised
- Disgusted

What other feelings can you feel in your body? Add those to the diagram on the next page as well.

You may want to make a copy of the drawings first, so you can have one diagram that shows ALL your feelings. Then, you can also try to make separate diagrams for each feeling.

FEELINGS IN MY BODY

· · · · · ·

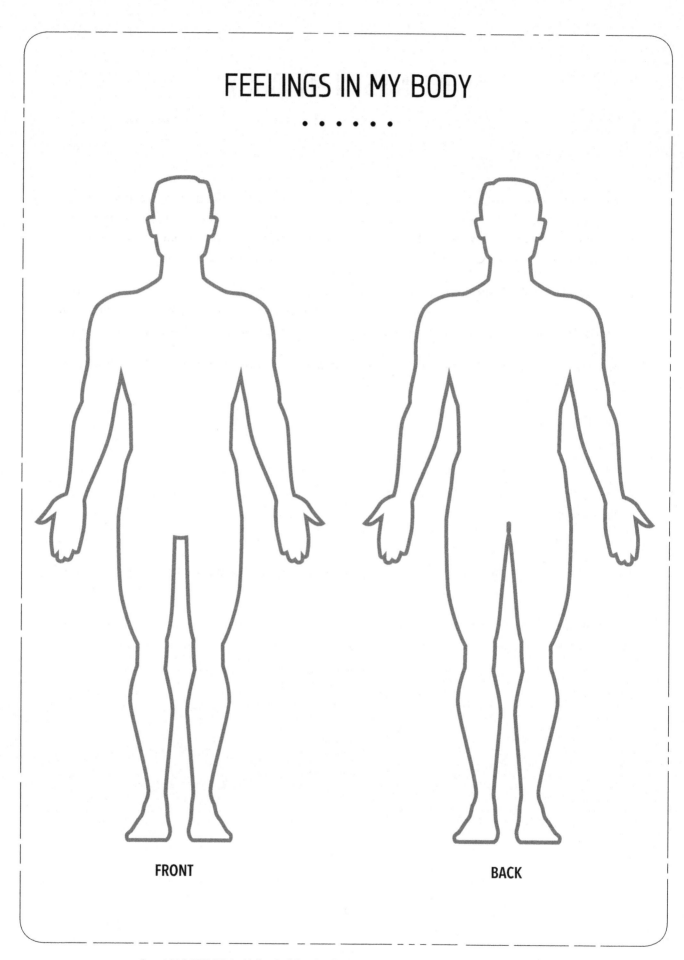

FRONT

BACK

PLAYING WITH FEELINGS

Feelings come in all shapes and sizes, and sometimes words don't really capture the true essence of a feeling. When you can't find the words to express your emotions, it can sometimes feel frustrating or you may even worry that there is something wrong with you.

It may help to know that many people have this experience at some point and for good reason: **Language and words are processed in a different part of your brain than emotions!** However, the connections between the language and feeling parts of your brain can be strengthened by practicing various ways of expressing and describing your feelings.

The exercises that follow will help your teen client to explore and express their feelings in different ways, some of which don't require any words at all. These exercises can help them to express feelings even when they don't have the words to do so. They can also help your clients to strengthen the connections between the thinking and feeling parts of their brain, which makes it easier to express their feelings over time.

As clients complete these exercises, please keep in mind that it does not matter how creative or artistic they might be. There is no right or wrong way to do these exercises. There is no grade at the end. They don't even have to ever show their work to anyone else in order to gain the benefits of the activities. The point of these exercises is to notice, observe, and express their feelings. It is the **process** – not the final product – that counts!

COLORFUL FEELINGS

· · · · · ·

At the most basic level, specific colors can remind us of specific feelings. For example, red may be associated with anger or love, and blue may remind you of sadness or calm.

For this exercise, you will need a variety of colors (markers, crayons, pencils, etc.). For each feeling word that is listed, select a color that reminds you of that feeling and add a bit of the color to the box.

Feel free to be as creative as you want when adding color to the box. For example, you may want to change the shape, texture, intensity, or form of the color to further convey the feeling.

Happy:	Sad:
Mad:	**Scared:**
Disgusted:	**Surprised:**
Other: _____	**Other:** _____

THE SOUNDTRACK OF MY LIFE

· · · · · · ·

Music has a great power to influence our mood, and it can also be used to express a variety of feelings. Our brains (and our emotions) are very responsive to sensory memories. In fact, our brains record and store all of our non-verbal memories, both positive and negative. That's why you might start smiling when you smell your favorite food: because your brain is remembering this as a positive sensory experience. The same is true for sound and music. Did you know that we usually pick out music to listen to that matches our mood? We can also change our mood by using a certain kind of music.

For each of the following feelings, please list a song that you associate with that feeling. It may be a song that makes you feel that emotion, a song that describes the way you experience that emotion, or a song that you like to listen to when you want to feel more of a certain emotion. At the bottom of the list, there is space for you to select a few additional emotions and select songs for those as well.

As you go through this exercise, you may find it helpful to listen to each song as you list it.

Happy: _____

Sad: _____

Mad: _____

Scared: _____

Disgusted: _____

Surprised: _____

_____: _____

_____: _____

_____: _____

_____: _____

EMOJI FEELINGS

· · · · · ·

Emojis are a fun way to express yourself without using any words. For each of these feelings, select at least 3 different emojis that represent that feeling for you. Challenge yourself to branch out beyond just the "faces" to more abstract images for some of the feelings. There are no right or wrong answers – the only goal is to see if you can express various feelings using an emoji vocabulary!

Happy:	Sad:
Mad:	**Scared:**
Disgusted:	**Surprised:**
Other: _____	**Other:** _____

LEARNING ABOUT TRIGGERS

• • • • • •

Sometimes, it seems like our feelings come out of nowhere, for no reason, and can take us by surprise. However, when we slow down and look at what is happening immediately before or when our feelings change, we often discover that our feelings are not so unpredictable. Rather, something has served to trigger that emotion in us. Triggers are those events, situations, people, or experiences that bring up specific feelings in us. Often, we think of triggers as those scenarios that elicit anger or sadness, but we also have triggers for positive emotions like happiness.

For each of the following feelings, list at least two situations that might trigger that emotion. For example, spending time with friends or eating a favorite meal may trigger happiness, whereas being alone or receiving a negative comment on social media might trigger sadness. If you can't think of any examples from your own life, you can use examples from books, television, movies, or situations that may have happened to a friend or family member.

In order to identify your triggers for each feeling, ask yourself these questions:

- Who makes me feel this way? (people)
- Where do I feel this way? (places)
- What am I thinking about when I have this feeling? (thoughts)
- What situations or activities normally make me feel this way? (situations)

Happy

Trigger: _____

Trigger: _____

Sad

Trigger: _____

Trigger: _____

Mad

Trigger: _____

Trigger: _____

Scared

Trigger: _____

Trigger: _____

Surprised

Trigger: _____

Trigger: _____

Disgusted

Trigger: _____

Trigger: _____

Other: _____

Trigger: _____

Trigger: _____

TRACKING MY TRIGGERS

· · · · · ·

Over the course of the next week, pay attention to your feelings and what is happening right before or when you have each feeling. **At the end of each day, write down one feeling and the trigger for that feeling**.

Monday

Feeling: _____

Trigger: _____

Tuesday

Feeling: _____

Trigger: _____

Wednesday

Feeling: _____

Trigger: _____

Thursday

Feeling: _____

Trigger: _____

Friday

Feeling: _____

Trigger: _____

Saturday

Feeling: _____

Trigger: _____

Sunday

Feeling: _____

Trigger: _____

At the end of the week, respond to the following questions:

For which feelings was it easiest to identify your triggers?

_____

_____

_____

For which feelings was it hardest to identify your triggers?

_____

_____

_____

Did you notice any patterns in your triggers over the course of the week?

_____

_____

_____

Were there any feelings that you avoided or neglected to track triggers for? Why do you think that might be?

_____

_____

_____

DISCOVERING THE DETAILS

· · · · · ·

Learning more about yourself will help you to know what situations trigger both positive and difficult emotions. **Use this worksheet to consider details of yourself that you may not have considered before.** Complete the following sentences with whatever comes to mind. Try not to overthink your responses, just write down the first answer you think of.

I am _____.

I like _____.

I wish _____.

I never _____.

I only _____.

I will _____.

I dream about _____.

I worry about _____.

I feel like _____.

I have trouble _____.

I am afraid of _____.

I am good at _____.

I can't stand _____.

I always _____.

I used to _____.

I don't believe _____.

_____ makes me happy.

_____ makes me laugh.

_____ makes me sad.

_____ makes me angry.

_____ frightens me.

_____ makes me worried.

CONNECTING MY FEELINGS AND TRIGGERS

• • • • • •

Being aware of triggers for your feelings is an important way that you can begin to manage your emotions. Despite the common experience that feelings just happen "for no reason," if you slow down and think about it, you can often identify a trigger for your feelings. Recognizing your triggers is a skill that you can develop with practice. Once you are able to identify triggers, you will be in a better position to identify ways to manage those triggers and, in turn, better manage your feelings.

For each of the following feelings, write down 3 situations, people, places, or other triggers that make you feel this way.

Happy:	Sad:
1.	1.
2.	2.
3.	3.
Mad:	**Scared:**
1.	1.
2.	2.
3.	3.
Disgusted:	**Surprised:**
1.	1.
2.	2.
3.	3.

LEARNING ABOUT ANXIETY

Anxiety is a common experience. In fact, in the United States, about 30% of all adolescents have an anxiety disorder. There are several different types of anxiety, which include some of the following:

- **Generalized Anxiety:** experiencing a lot of worry about a variety of different things, which gets in the way of living your daily life
- **Phobias:** extreme fear about something specific (e.g., fear of spiders), when the fear is greater than the actual threat
- **Panic:** a panic attack involves multiple physical symptoms and a feeling of being overwhelmed by fear or dread

When we feel anxiety, our body and mind are responding to a perceived threat, whether that threat is real or imagined. The threat can be physical, emotional, or just based on our thoughts. Indeed, many times, people have the experience of anxiety even when there is no real threat in the present moment.

There are several situations that can cause us to experience anxiety. For one, we can experience anxiety when we imagine something that makes us afraid or uncomfortable, even if we know it's not real. For example, you might see a scary movie about aliens and later imagine that aliens are going to invade your house – even though you know that is not really going to happen! Similarly, waking up from a bad dream, watching upsetting stories on the news, or worrying about your upcoming final exams are all situations that may spark the feeling of anxiety.

There's a particular part of our brain – called the limbic system – that stores all of our non-verbal (aka sensory) memories. The limbic system also contains the amygdala, which is responsible for detecting emotions like fear and anxiety. The amygdala functions similar to a fire alarm in that it serves as an "early warning system" in case of potential threat or danger. When the amygdala gets triggered (just like pulling the handle on a fire alarm), the internal parts of our brain respond with their version of lights and sirens. Once those warning signals have started, our body may feel a variety of different physical sensations, and the thinking part of our brain – called the prefrontal cortex – may have a harder time determining if the danger is real or not. The following is a list of what some of these physical sensations may involve.

Physical Symptoms Associated with Anxiety

- Increased heart rate
- Feeling like you are going to vomit
- Feeling like your heart is going to burst
- Muscle tension
- Stomachache
- Headache
- Feelings of fatigue
- Difficulty sleeping
- Difficulty concentrating
- Shaking or trembling
- Feeling like your legs are weak
- Feeling like you might faint
- Avoiding things that make you feel nervous, afraid, or worried

EXPLORING ANXIETY

· · · · · ·

Everyone experiences anxiety; it is a natural part of being human. This worksheet will help you to better understand your own anxiety and begin to find ways to manage those feelings when you have them.

List the things, circumstances, or thoughts that make you anxious or nervous.

1. _____

2. _____

3. _____

4. _____

5. _____

6. _____

Now go back and rate them all, using #1 for the hardest situation and #6 for the easiest to manage. Pick a situation that you labeled as #1 or #2 (one of your hardest, most anxiety-provoking situations) and answer the following questions with that situation in mind:

What are some of the thoughts or worries you have in this situation? (Thoughts might include things like: I am going to fail, I am going to be rejected, I am going to get in trouble, or I am (or someone I love is) going to get seriously hurt or sick.)

_____

_____

_____

What are some of the feelings (emotional and physical) you have in this situation? (Physical feelings might include: nausea, tightening in your chest, knots in your stomach, or tingling hands or feet. Emotional feelings might include: irritation, anger, embarrassment, or fear.)

_____

_____

_____

Now, consider *all* of the situations you previously listed that make you anxious, as well as any other situations you can think of.

How do you respond when you are feeling anxious in these situations? What actions do you usually take?

_____

_____

_____

Think about the ways in which anxiety has had an effect on your life. Are there activities you would like to do but don't? Friendships, relationships, or jobs that have been impacted? Write about 3 (or more) ways that anxiety has impacted you.

_____

_____

_____

Imagine that tomorrow you wake up and all your anxiety is gone. What would be different in your life?

1. _____

_____

2. _____

_____

3. _____

_____

What are some steps you can imagine doing to take charge and change your anxiety?

_____

_____

Who would be a good support person for you when you start taking charge of your anxiety?

_____

_____

UNDERSTANDING MY ANXIETY

· · · · · · ·

On the "Exploring Anxiety" worksheet, you identified several situations that make you anxious. Use the chart to look at those situations a little more closely. **For each situation, fill out the chart to identify the feelings (physical sensations and emotions), thoughts and worries, and actions that most often accompany that situation.** Then, imagine how you would like to handle the situation, and fill in the final column for what you wish would happen in that situation. Don't worry about whether or not you believe that you can achieve that outcome. Just focus on imagining a more desirable outcome for the situation.

Situation	What I feel (Physical sensations and emotions)	What I think (Thoughts and worries)	What I do (Actions)	What I wish would happen
1.				
2.				
3.				

CHECKING OUT THE FACTS

. . . . . .

Worries are thoughts that lead to anxious feelings. One way to manage anxiety is to challenge your worry thoughts. **Use the following questions to try out this anxiety management strategy.**

What are you worried about?

_____

_____

_____

What evidence do you have that it will come true?

_____

_____

_____

What's the *worst* that could happen if it did come true?

_____

_____

_____

What's most likely to happen if your worry does come true?

_____

_____

_____

What are the chances that you will be okay (in a week, a month, a year)?

_____

_____

_____

TRACKING MY ANXIETY TRIGGERS

· · · · · ·

Over the course of the next week, pay attention to your feelings and what is happening right before or when you experience anxiety. At the end of each day, write down one anxiety trigger, and rate the intensity of your anxiety on a scale of 1–10 (with 1 being not anxious at all, and 10 being the highest possible level of anxiety).

Monday

Trigger: _____

Anxiety Rating: _____

Tuesday

Trigger: _____

Anxiety Rating: _____

Wednesday

Trigger: _____

Anxiety Rating: _____

Thursday

Trigger: _____

Anxiety Rating: _____

Friday

Trigger: _____

Anxiety Rating: _____

Saturday

Trigger: _____

Anxiety Rating: _____

Sunday

Trigger: _____

Anxiety Rating: _____

ANXIETY THERMOMETER

· · · · · ·

Using a thermometer is one way to measure how intense a certain feeling is at any given time. Think about your anxiety when you use the following thermometer.

As you think about your anxiety, see if you can think of words that describe how the anxiety feels at 25, 50, 75, and 100% intensity. For example, 25% might be "A little uncomfortable," 50% might be "Hard but tolerable," 75% might be "Really uncomfortable," and 100% could be "Overwhelmed." For each of these intensities, please note how you notice the anxiety in your body. For example, when some people feel anxious, they may feel their heart rate increase and notice energy in their arms and legs.

Once you have filled in your thermometer, you can use it at any time to assess how you are feeling with regard to your anxiety.

— 100%

— 75%

— 50%

— 25%

Anxiety

At 100% I feel: _____

My body cues are: _____

At 75% I feel: _____

My body cues are: _____

At 50% I feel: _____

My body cues are: _____

At 25% I feel: _____

My body cues are: _____

SOCIAL ANXIETY

Social anxiety occurs when ordinary, day-to-day social situations cause extreme discomfort, anxiety, or self-consciousness. It involves feeling nervous or embarrassed when other people are looking at you – or when you think they might be looking at you.

Everyone experiences at least some mild anxiety about social situations at some point in their life. Starting at a new school, joining a club, or going to a dance are all common situations in which people often feel slightly uncomfortable. However, people with social anxiety experience a significant amount of discomfort or anxiety that is much greater than average. Since everyone is different, the situations or circumstances that are challenging for your client might not be the same for their sibling or friends. **The following are examples of social situations that might cause someone to become socially anxious:**

- Meeting someone new
- Speaking in front of the class
- Talking to someone in authority
- Going to a concert or other large event
- Going to the mall

EXPLORING SOCIAL ANXIETY

• • • • • •

Everyone experiences social anxiety at some point in their life. This worksheet will help you identify and better understand the situations that cause you social anxiety, and explore ways to manage these feelings when they arise.

List the social situations that make you anxious or uncomfortable.

1. _____

2. _____

3. _____

4. _____

5. _____

6. _____

Now go back and rate them all, using #1 for the hardest situation and #6 for the easiest to manage. Pick a situation that you labeled as #1 or #2 (one of your hardest, most anxiety-provoking situations) and answer the following questions with that situation in mind:

What are some of the thoughts or worries you have in this situation? (Thoughts might include things like: I will be embarrassed, be rejected, look foolish, draw attention to myself, or not know what to say.)

_____

_____

_____

What are some of the feelings (emotional and physical) you have in this situation? Physical feelings might include: nausea, tightening in your chest, stomach knots, or tingling hands or feet. Emotional feelings might include: irritation, anger, embarrassment, or fear.

_____

_____

_____

Now, consider *all* of the situations you previously listed that cause social anxiety, as well as any others you can think of, and respond to the following questions:

How do you respond when you are feeling socially anxious? What actions do you usually take?

_____

_____

_____

Think about the ways in which social anxiety has had an effect on your life. Are there activities you would like to do but don't? Friendships, relationships, or jobs that have been impacted? Write a paragraph about 3 (or more) ways social anxiety has impacted you.

_____

_____

_____

Imagine that tomorrow you woke up and all your social anxiety was gone. What would be different in your life?

1. _____

_____

2. _____

_____

3. _____

_____

Imagine yourself like a butterfly. What two actions can you take this week to begin to fly free from your social anxiety?

1. _____

_____

2. _____

_____

UNDERSTANDING MY SOCIAL ANXIETY

· · · · · · ·

On the "Exploring Social Anxiety" worksheet, you identified several situations that make you socially anxious. Use the chart below to look at those situations a little more closely. **For each situation, fill out the chart to identify the feelings (physical sensations and emotions), thoughts and worries, and actions that most often accompany that situation.** Then, imagine how you would like to handle the situation, and fill in the final column for what you wish would happen in that situation. Don't worry about whether or not you believe that you can achieve that outcome. Just focus on imagining a more desirable outcome for the situation.

Situation	What I feel (Physical sensations and emotions)	What I think (Thoughts and worries)	What I do (Actions)	What I wish would happen
1.				
2.				
3.				

2

COGNITIVE SKILLS

Working from a trauma-informed approach requires an understanding of the impact of trauma and the use of strategies that minimize the potential for re-traumatization. Adolescents who have experienced any of the traumas described in the introduction of this workbook are at risk for a multitude of long-term effects. As one example, early life adversities can have an impact on the cognitive development of the adolescent. In particular, adolescents who have experienced trauma may exhibit potential delays or deficits in their general cognitive skills, language, memory, executive functioning, or ability to process social and emotional information (McLean, 2016). Some studies have found a link between exposure to trauma and decreased verbal IQ in adolescents, as well as lower performance on a number of different memory-related tasks in teens who have experienced trauma.

One way that trauma affects adolescent cognitive development is through its impact on the brain's neural circuitry. Traumatic events alter the ways in which a teenager's neural pathways develop, and these pathways, in turn, form the basis from which they view and perceive the world. Therefore, adolescents who have been exposed to trauma develop neural pathways in which the world is viewed from a lens of threat, danger, and injustice. However, the human brain is malleable, and its underlying neural circuitry does not have to stay permanently "hardwired," so to speak. This is particularly true in adolescence, when the brain is still developing and forming new connections all the time. **Therefore, even teenagers who have been exposed to trauma can still develop new, more adaptive neural pathways throughout the course of treatment. The brain's amazing ability to adapt and change (what has been termed "neuroplasticity") allows for the opportunity to develop different cognitive pathways that support recovery and growth.** Given this, one important aspect of trauma-informed treatment involves providing teenagers a framework that addresses the cognitive impact of trauma.

Effective clinical treatment for addressing the cognitive impact of trauma utilizes the fundamental principles that characterize a cognitive (or cognitive-behavioral) framework. The goal of cognitive therapy is to provide the client "strategies to evaluate their thinking and manage problematic behaviors" (Association for Behavioral and Cognitive Therapies, 2018). One particular goal of treatment is to help teens understand how their core beliefs and thinking errors shape their perspective and understanding of the world, which allows them to begin to develop a different "operating system." By using disputation strategies to challenge these underlying assumptions about themselves and others (in the context of a safe environment), the teen can begin to develop new neural pathways that support a healthier lifestyle and self-concept. Indeed, research has demonstrated the effectiveness of cognitive-behavioral treatment in children and adolescents who have experienced trauma (Meiser-Stedman et al., 2016), including evidence for reductions in anxiety, emotional difficulties, depression, and conduct problems.

HOW TO INCORPORATE THE COGNITIVE SKILLS WORKSHEETS

This workbook focuses specifically on addressing cognitive skills within the framework of a trauma-informed approach to treatment. **The worksheets in this section cover basic cognitive skills, including labeling and identifying thought patterns, as well as understanding the difference between worry and anxiety. Worksheets are also included regarding basic thinking errors and how adolescents can more easily identify these errors throughout the course of their daily lives.**

While the specific exercises in this section may be familiar to the clinician, they are meant to be used in conjunction with the exercises on basic emotion skills (Chapter 1), the body's response to trauma (Chapter 3), self-regulation (Chapter 4), increasing positive feelings (Chapter 5), meaning making after trauma (Chapter 7), and safety (Chapter 8). Of course, the information in this chapter can be used as a specific intervention to support cognitive and behavioral change. However, we especially recommend including the material on basic emotion skills as a preliminary approach prior to working on cognitive skills, given that many adolescents are prone to experience some resistance to interventions that appear "academically oriented." In addition, we believe that building the teen's sense of safety and developing a strong therapeutic relationship enhances their ability to utilize cognitive skills on a more regular basis. Working to establish a positive connection with the teen can be facilitated by discussing of areas of interest (e.g., music, sports, video games), and then using these topics as a jumping-off point for work on basic emotion (and, subsequently, cognitive) skills.

One stumbling block in addressing cognitions for many teenagers is that they often experience difficulty in identifying the underlying fears and core beliefs that fuel their negative automatic thoughts. In addition, adolescents are often reluctant to shift their mindset and incorporate new perspectives simply based on the suggestion of an adult, particularly one in a position of some authority. To overcome these barriers, it can be incredibly helpful for the adolescent to get feedback from their peers so they can hear examples of times in which challenging and altering belief systems resulted in positive change. For example, if a student hears from a classmate that he was "certain" he had failed an exam – and then the classmate shares how his teacher helped him see this was an assumption, rather than a fact – then the original student may begin to have some hope that the "worst case scenario" is not always a foregone conclusion.

As much as possible, we also encourage clinicians to utilize real-world examples of how to dispute and challenge thinking errors. For example, the clinician can discuss a hypothetical situation in which a female teenager has developed a belief system that she is unattractive and will never have friends. Helping guide the teenager through the steps of a disputation process for this fictional (yet common) example, the clinician can support the teen in figuring out ways to test the theory, determine possible alternative options for the hypothetical teen to take, and draw upon the teen's own personal and peer experiences to suggest potential solutions. Incorporating concrete examples to which teenagers can relate not only supports the development of the therapeutic relationship, but it also helps increase adolescents' understanding of the connection between their thoughts, feelings, and behaviors. Asking teens for examples from their life (or their friends' lives) is another strategy that allows you to use situations that are relevant and specific to them. It's often easier to use an example of a thinking error that is being experienced by a teen's friend – and which the teen can identify as being false – so the teen can get used to how the disputation process works. This strategy also sidesteps the natural resistance and defensiveness that teens experience when their own underlying assumptions are challenged.

THOUGHTS VS. FEELINGS

· · · · · · ·

Thoughts and feelings are related, but they are not the same.

Feelings arise from the physiological reactions that occur in our body. The feeling of excitement may be experienced as energy in your arms and legs, an increased heart rate, or butterflies in your stomach.

Thoughts, on the other hand, are the judgments, interpretations, and values that we use to understand our feelings and experiences. Thoughts make up the internal dialogue in your mind. When you feel excitement, you may think that something positive is about to happen or you may think that you have done a good job.

The distinction between thoughts and feelings can get tricky because people often express their thoughts by saying "I feel…" For example, someone might say, "I feel that we should do this and not that." In this case, the person is using "I feel" as a thought – not a feeling – because it involves the individual's judgment or opinion about the situation, not their physiological or emotional reaction. When people use "I feel" in this context, what they mean to say is "I believe that…" or "I think that…"

Use the following worksheet to practice identifying thoughts vs. feelings.

THOUGHTS VS. FEELINGS

· · · · · ·

The following exercise will help you practice identifying thoughts and feelings.

For each item, select whether it is a *thought* or a *feeling*:	Thought	Feeling
1. I feel calm.		
2. I feel like things will never get better.		
3. I feel like I am a loser.		
4. I feel depressed.		
5. I feel rejected.		
6. I feel helpless.		
7. I feel happy.		
8. I feel sad.		
9. I feel like you shouldn't be rude.		
10. I feel like you are making the wrong choice.		
11. I feel unloved.		
12. I feel left out.		
13. I feel like this is unfair.		
14. I feel unsure.		
15. I feel like you don't love me.		

ANXIETY OR WORRY?

· · · · · ·

People often use the words anxiety and worry interchangeably. Although the two constructs are related, there is an important difference between them.

Anxiety is your body's physiological and emotional reaction to stress or danger. Anxiety is a *feeling*.

Worry, on the other hand, consists of the thoughts, judgments, or interpretations of the situation that is causing you anxiety. In other words, worry has to do with the words you say to yourself when you are anxious. Worries are *thoughts*.

Here are some things to keep in mind about anxiety and worry:

1. Worry and anxiety can be experienced together or separately.
2. Worry is experienced in your head; anxiety is experienced in your body.
3. Worry tends to be specific, whereas anxiety is generally a full-body feeling.

The following activity will help you distinguish anxiety from worry and understand how they are related.

1. Imagine that you are about to take a very hard test at school in a subject that you find very difficult.

   Anxiety:

   What feelings would you have about this situation?

   _____

   _____

   How would you recognize these feelings in your body?

   _____

   _____

   Worry:

   What thoughts might be in your mind?

   _____

   _____

What might you say to yourself or someone else about this situation?

_____

_____

2. Pretend that you are about to have a very important interview. This interview could be for a job that you want, a school that you would like to attend, or a team sport you would like to participate in. Imagine that you have wanted this opportunity for a long time and that it is very important to you.

Anxiety:

What feelings would you have about this situation?

_____

_____

How would you recognize these feelings in your body?

_____

_____

Worry:

What thoughts might be in your mind?

_____

_____

What might you say to yourself or someone else about this situation?

_____

_____

WORRY LOG

· · · · · ·

Sometimes, we have numerous things that we worry about. Sometimes, it's just one or two things, but we think about them a LOT. Some worries don't bother us too much, and other worries bring up really strong feelings of anxiety. One of the ways that you can start dealing with worries is to identify *what* they are. Remember that worries are *thoughts*, while anxiety is a *feeling*. Once you identify your worry thoughts, you can decide if it's something that warrants your concern, and if so, you can make a plan to address the concern.

For the next week, keep track of the worries that you have. Write down at least two worries that you have each day, whether they are big or small. For each worry, rate how much anxiety the worry causes you using the following scale:

1	2	3	4	5	6	7	8	9	10
Not at all anxious			Somewhat anxious			Very anxious			Extremely anxious

Remember: Worries are thoughts, whereas anxiety involves physical and emotional feelings!

Day 1	Worry 1:	Anxiety Rating:
	Worry 2:	Anxiety Rating:
Day 2	Worry 1:	Anxiety Rating:
	Worry 2:	Anxiety Rating:

Day 3	Worry 1:	Anxiety Rating:
	Worry 2:	Anxiety Rating:
Day 4	Worry 1:	Anxiety Rating:
	Worry 2:	Anxiety Rating:
Day 5	Worry 1:	Anxiety Rating:
	Worry 2:	Anxiety Rating:
Day 6	Worry 1:	Anxiety Rating:
	Worry 2:	Anxiety Rating:
Day 7	Worry 1:	Anxiety Rating:
	Worry 2:	Anxiety Rating:

THOUGHTS, FEELINGS, & BEHAVIORS

• • • • • •

In any given situation, we have thoughts, feelings, and behaviors:

Thoughts are the words that you say to yourself (aka your internal dialogue).

Feelings are the physiological and emotional reactions in your body.

Behaviors are the actions that you take or the things that you do.

Thoughts, feelings, and behaviors are all related and can influence each other. Think of this like the three arms of a triangle. You can start with any of the three sides, and there's a connected reaction in the other two sides. When we think something, this has an impact on how we feel, and how we feel influences the way we behave.

It works the same way if you start with a behavior: Your action results in both thoughts and feelings about that. Keep in mind that, sometimes, your response is that you *don't* take an action, but you still have feelings and thoughts about the behavior of *not acting*.

In the following section, we will go over some examples of how thoughts, feelings, and actions influence each other and are connected.

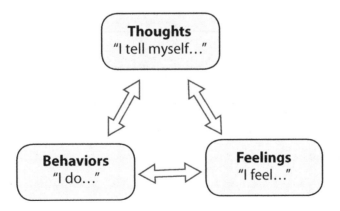

Situation: Sam got a C- on a math test.

Thoughts

- I am going to fail this class.
- I will never get into college.
- My parents are going to be so mad at me.
- I'm so stupid.

Behaviors

- Avoids telling parents about the test grade.
- Doesn't talk to the teacher for help.

Feelings

- Anxiety
- Stomachache
- Clenched jaw

How might Sam's thoughts and feelings have influenced his behaviors in this situation?

_____

_____

_____

Because thoughts, feelings, and behaviors are all connected, a change in any one of these areas can influence the others. Changing thoughts is a powerful and simple (although not always easy) way that you can change your feelings and behaviors.

A simple strategy to evaluate your thoughts is to ask yourself:

- **T:** Is this thought **T**rue?
- **H:** Is this thought **H**elpful?
- **I:** Is this thought **I**nspiring?
- **N:** Is this thought **N**ecessary?
- **K:** Is this thought **K**ind?

Let's look back at Sam's thoughts when he got the C- on his math test:

- "I am going to fail this class."
- "I will never get into college."
- "My parents are going to be so mad at me."
- "I'm so stupid."

Are these thoughts **true**? Are these the only possible outcomes?

_____

_____

Are these thoughts **helpful**? Does thinking this way help Sam towards his goal of passing the math class?

_____

_____

Are these thoughts **inspiring**? Do these thoughts motivate Sam to do better next time?

_____

_____

Are these thoughts **necessary**? Which of Sam's thoughts was least helpful in this situation?

_____

_____

Are these thoughts **kind**? Is this the way you would speak to a friend in the same situation?

_____

_____

What are some different ways Sam could think about this situation that would be more true, helpful, inspiring, necessary, and kind?

1. _____

2. _____

3. _____

4. _____

Now, let's look at how Sam's situation might be different if he were to replace his unhelpful, negative thoughts with more helpful or positive thoughts:

Thoughts

- I am going to need to work harder to learn these concepts.

- I still have time to get my grade up before the end of the semester.

Behaviors

- Asks his teacher for help with the problems he doesn't understand.

- Tells his parents that he is worried about his math class grade this semester.

Feelings

- Anxiety

- Butterflies in stomach

Notice that while Sam still feels anxious, his changes in thinking have led to different behaviors.

How might these behaviors lead to more positive outcomes for Sam?

_____

_____

_____

Let's apply this concept to a situation in your life. Think of a recent situation that was moderately stressful for you. Fill in the following chart to show what your thoughts, feelings, and behaviors were in this situation.

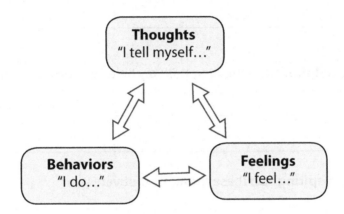

Situation: _____

My thoughts:

1. _____

2. _____

3. _____

My feelings:

1. _____

2. _____

3. _____

My behaviors:

1. _____

2. _____

3. _____

Now, let's evaluate how helpful your thoughts were in this situation:

Are these thoughts **true**? Are these the only possible outcomes?

_____

_____

Are these thoughts **helpful**? Does thinking this way help you towards your goal?

_____

_____

Are these thoughts **inspiring**? Do these thoughts motivate you?

_____

_____

Are these thoughts **necessary**? Which of your thoughts were least helpful in this situation?

_____

_____

Are these thoughts **kind**? Is this the way you would speak to a friend in the same situation?

_____

_____

Which of your thoughts could you change to be more helpful or positive in this situation?

1. Old thought:

_____

Replacement thought:

_____

2. Old thought:

_____

Replacement thought:

_____

3. Old thought:

_____

Replacement thought:

_____

How might changing your thoughts in this situation lead to different feelings?

_____

_____

_____

How could different thoughts and feelings change your behaviors? Could the outcome of this situation have been any different if your behaviors were different?

_____

_____

_____

THOUGHT LOG

· · · · · ·

The following activity will help you to more easily identify how thoughts, feelings, and behaviors are connected with one another. In this activity, you will track your thoughts, feelings, and behaviors over the course of one week.

Each day, record at least two situations that occurred, as well as what you thought, how you felt, and what you did in response to the situation. You can record any type of situation – it can be positive, boring, stressful – whatever you choose. You will be identifying the thoughts, feelings, and behaviors associated with each situation you pick.

Day 1:

Situation	Thoughts	Feelings	Behaviors
	1. 2.	1. 2.	1. 2.
	1. 2.	1. 2.	1. 2.

Day 2:

Situation	Thoughts	Feelings	Behaviors
	1. 2.	1. 2.	1. 2.
	1. 2.	1. 2.	1. 2.

Day 3:

Situation	Thoughts	Feelings	Behaviors
	1. 2.	1. 2.	1. 2.
	1. 2.	1. 2.	1. 2.

Day 4:

Situation	Thoughts	Feelings	Behaviors
	1. 2.	1. 2.	1. 2.
	1. 2.	1. 2.	1. 2.

Day 5:

Situation	Thoughts	Feelings	Behaviors
	1. 2.	1. 2.	1. 2.
	1. 2.	1. 2.	1. 2.

Day 6:

Situation	Thoughts	Feelings	Behaviors
	1. 2.	1. 2.	1. 2.
	1. 2.	1. 2.	1. 2.

Day 7:

Situation	Thoughts	Feelings	Behaviors
	1. 2.	1. 2.	1. 2.
	1. 2.	1. 2.	1. 2.

At the end of the week, respond to the following questions:

What thoughts were true, helpful, inspiring, necessary, and kind?

_____

_____

_____

What thoughts were **NOT** true, helpful, inspiring, necessary and kind?

_____

_____

_____

How did your thoughts impact your feelings?

_____

_____

_____

How did your thoughts and feelings impact your behavior?

_____

_____

_____

What is one situation that occurred this week when your thoughts could have been more true, helpful, inspiring, necessary, and kind?

_____

_____

_____

What replacement thoughts would have been more positive in this situation?

_____

_____

_____

How do you think the situation might have been different if you had changed your thoughts?

_____

_____

_____

WHY WE CAN'T ALWAYS BELIEVE
OUR OWN THOUGHTS

· · · · · ·

DON'T BELIEVE EVERYTHING YOU THINK.

Just like your body has certain patterns of actions and responses, so does your mind. Our brains are generating thoughts all the time. If you doubt this, try paying attention to what goes through your head while you are showering. You will be amazed at the different, random things you think – even when you are just having a conversation with yourself!

Our ability to think is a good thing, but that doesn't mean that everything we think is true and/or accurate. Indeed, sometimes the things we think can actually increase our experience of anxiety or make it more likely that we will feel anxious! One reason for this is that our brains are wired to pay more attention to the negative (or the possibility that something will be negative) as part of our survival mechanism. This is great in terms of alerting us to real, present dangers. However, this also means that we are more likely to generate thoughts about *perceived* dangers that aren't based in fact, which can cause use to experience anxiety.

Patterns of thinking that lead to increased anxiety are called **thinking errors**, and they are distorted (or inaccurate) ways of thinking. Although there is a group of common "thinking errors" that all human beings tend to make, this doesn't mean that you are engaging in all of these, all the time. Rather, it means that we all have times when we get caught up in a certain way of thinking, and it helps to check to make sure that we are being objective and neutral, rather than stuck in a negative pattern of thinking (Burns, 1989).

Here are the most common thinking errors:

1. **All-or-Nothing Thinking:** Tending to see things as awesome or terrible and missing out on all the possible "shades of gray" in between. For example, you're on the basketball team and you're playing in a game. You make seven baskets, but you miss one time and don't score. You think that you had a "terrible" game because of the one missed attempt and don't give yourself credit for the seven times you did score.

2. **Overgeneralization:** Taking one outcome and thinking that it accurately predicts every similar future experience. For example, you get a low grade on one test and think that this means you will automatically fail the class.

3. **Mental Filter:** Taking one piece of information (that you see as negative) and leaving out or ignoring all of the additional positive pieces of information related to the situation. This can look a lot like overgeneralization. For example, the teacher calls on you in class and you don't know the answer to the question. You see yourself as "stupid" and believe you are failing the class, even though you have gotten really good grades on your tests and quizzes in the class, and you usually know the answers when the teacher calls on you.

4. **Disqualifying the Positive:** Acknowledging that something was positive but immediately deciding that it *doesn't count as much* as the perceived negative experience. For example, you get a good grade on a paper but decide that the teacher must have given everyone an A (because you believe the teacher doesn't think you are capable of doing "good" work).

5. **Mind Reading:** Believing you know what someone else is thinking even though they haven't actually said or done something that makes it clear. For example, you see someone frowning while you pass them in the hallway and believe that their frown is directed at you because they don't like you.

6. **Jumping to Conclusions/Fortune Telling:** Coming to a conclusion or predicting an outcome about something with no real evidence that it is true. For example, you believe that you will never have a relationship because you haven't gone out with someone in the last few months.

7. **Catastrophizing or Minimization:** Seeing things as worse than they are (catastrophizing) OR seeing things as less important or worthwhile than they are (minimizing a positive accomplishment). For example, you text your friend (who usually answers pretty quickly) and you don't hear back from her for several hours, so you believe she is mad at you and won't want to talk to you anymore.

8. **Emotional Reasoning:** Believing that your emotions accurately reflect the truth of a situation. For example, you feel lonely and believe this is because no one likes you.

9. **Should Statements:** Having a set of expectations about yourself or someone else that "should" be met – and then feeling guilty or angry when those expectations aren't met. For example, thinking that you "should" be exercising every single day and then feeling guilty and bad on days you don't exercise.

10. **Labeling:** Taking an overgeneralization and adding a label (usually a negative one) to it. For example, you don't know the answer to a question in class and decide that you are "an idiot" or "stupid."

11. **Personalization:** Feeling like you are to blame for anything or everything that doesn't go right. For example, you feel like you are the reason your parent says he or she has a headache.

Which thinking errors can you identify having used over the last week?

_____

_____

_____

Which thinking error seems to be the one you fall into the most?

_____

_____

_____

Which thinking error would you like to change in your life first? Why?

_____

_____

_____

CHALLENGING THINKING ERRORS

• • • • • •

One of the best ways to combat thinking errors is called **disputation**. This is a process in which you check out the facts about your thoughts regarding the situation. You take the position of being neutral, such as imagining yourself as a scientist testing a hypothesis or a detective solving a mystery. Let's use the *personalization* example described earlier: You think it's your fault that your mother has a headache. First, you have to gather the evidence, the facts that you have about the situation. In this case, the facts might be as follows: 1) Your mother has a headache, 2) she told you she woke up with the headache, and 3) she has had many headaches before.

Now, let's try to come up with theories, or possible reasons why your mother has had a headache. Your initial theory is that it's because of you. Some other theories might be: 1) Your mother has allergies that cause headaches, 2) your mother was up late last night finishing a project for work, or 3) your mother is trying to give up caffeine and hasn't had any coffee for a day.

Next, look at your theories and see if there are any facts that you forgot to include when you were gathering the evidence. In this case, you add allergies, staying up late, and giving up caffeine to your list of facts, since all of those are true. Now, let's consider the evidence that your mother's headache is "because of you." What evidence might support that theory? You are not responsible for her allergies, or her decision to give up caffeine. You did ask your mom for help with a project last night, and that may have meant she stayed up later than usual. However, your mom made her own choice to help you and to keep working past her usual bedtime.

What's an alternative conclusion that you could draw from the evidence you've collected? You might think that your mom has a headache related to a combination of allergies and lack of caffeine (headaches are a really common symptom of both of these). When your mom has had headaches before, did it only happen when you asked her for help? Perhaps you remember that she also has more headaches in the spring, when there's a lot of pollen in the air.

Now, compare the evidence that her headache is "because of you" against the evidence that something else caused the headache (such as allergies or no coffee). **This is the process of disputation, as you look at the evidence, the possible theories, and determine which explanation fits the facts**. In this case, there is no evidence that you "caused" her headache, and there are several pieces of evidence that this is a physical condition that is not your fault (or your responsibility).

Let's look at one more example, from *all-or-nothing thinking*. In this example, you believe that you performed "horribly" during the basketball game. Gathering the evidence, these are the facts of the situation: 1) You scored seven times, 2) you missed one basket, and 3) your coach kept you in the game the whole time. What other evidence might you consider? 1) You tried your best while playing, 2) most professional basketball players miss shots during a game, and 3) the coach gives very little playing time to players who aren't working hard. These are other factors to consider that are important to address this issue.

Your theory is that missing one basket means you did a horrible job during the game. What is an alternative theory based on the evidence? Your performance during the game resulted in making seven baskets and staying on the court, which is evidence of playing well. It's true that you missed one shot, but overall you did a great job. Paying attention to your accomplishments (and not just the missed opportunity) in a balanced way gives a very different conclusion.

Along with looking at the facts of the circumstances, you can also challenge thinking errors by determining the likelihood, or **probability**, of the negative outcome. Probability is different from possibility. Sometimes, people argue a point by saying, "You can't know that – it's *possible* that it could happen." While it's true that something may be possible, that is very different from it being highly likely, or probable, to occur.

For example, you read a story about a bus that broke down in a snowstorm, and you begin to worry that *your* bus will also break down in a snowstorm. While it is technically possible that could occur, you live in a state that hasn't had more than an inch of snow since you've lived there (and you have been there your whole life). Therefore, there is a very *low probability* that there will be a large snowstorm in your town, and it's even less likely that you would be on a bus that breaks down in a snowstorm (since there is a *high probability* that school would be cancelled if it ever did snow).

Another example of this would be a situation in which you forget to turn in your homework for one class, on one day, and you begin to believe that you will not graduate, never get a job, and be homeless. While there is a *tiny possibility* that all of those things could come true, it's not very likely. If you regularly do your homework, study for your tests, and are passing all of your classes, then there is a very *high probability* that you will graduate, even if you missed one homework assignment.

IDENTIFYING THINKING ERRORS

• • • • • •

In this exercise, you will practice how to be a thinking error detective, using situations that have already happened in your life. You might want to start with a situation in which you felt a little unhappy or displeased, as opposed to extremely upset. You can work up to using situations that felt more important or more upsetting.

Go back to the list of thinking errors that you already identified and fill out the chart with information regarding the situation, what you thought at the time, and the type of thinking error. Then, try to come up with an alternative thought, based on your detective process. A sample scenario using the previous headache example is provided for you.

Situation	What I Thought	Type of Thinking Error	Alternative Thought
Mom has a headache.	It's because of me.	Personalization	Mom's headache is from physical issues (allergies and/or lack of caffeine).

CHANGING THOUGHTS LOG

. . . . . .

In this activity, you will track your thoughts, feelings, and behaviors over the course of one week. This activity is intended to help you see the ways in which your thoughts, feelings, and behaviors are connected. This is also a way in which you can add in your detective skills and keep improving your ability to consider alternative explanations. As you practice doing this, you will be able to see the patterns in your thoughts and will be able to develop a new, more balanced way of thinking about the situations in your life. Remember that our thoughts, feelings, and behaviors are like the three sides of a triangle. When we change our thoughts, we are also able to change our feelings and behaviors.

Each day, record one situation that occurred, as well as what you thought, how you felt, and what you did in response to the situation. We usually don't struggle a lot with the positive connections between thoughts, feelings, and actions, so start with a situation that you found challenging or stressful. Make sure to identify the specifics of the situation and how you originally thought, felt, and acted. Then, consider what might have been a different way to think about the situation.

Write down some possible alternative, more helpful thoughts that you could have used in this situation, and the likely feelings, behaviors, and outcomes that would have resulted from those thoughts.

Day 1:_____

Situation	Original Thoughts	Original Feelings	Original Behaviors
	1. 2.	1. 2.	1. 2.
	Alternative Thoughts	**Possible Feelings**	**Possible Behaviors**
	1. 2.	1. 2.	1. 2.

Day 2: _____

Situation	Original Thoughts	Original Feelings	Original Behaviors
	1. 2.	1. 2.	1. 2.
	Alternative Thoughts	**Possible Feelings**	**Possible Behaviors**
	1. 2.	1. 2.	1. 2.

Day 3: _____

Situation	Original Thoughts	Original Feelings	Original Behaviors
	1. 2.	1. 2.	1. 2.
	Alternative Thoughts	**Possible Feelings**	**Possible Behaviors**
	1. 2.	1. 2.	1. 2.

Day 4: _____

Situation	Original Thoughts	Original Feelings	Original Behaviors
	1. 2.	1. 2.	1. 2.
	Alternative Thoughts	**Possible Feelings**	**Possible Behaviors**
	1. 2.	1. 2.	1. 2.

Day 5: _____

Situation	Original Thoughts	Original Feelings	Original Behaviors
	1. 2.	1. 2.	1. 2.
	Alternative Thoughts	**Possible Feelings**	**Possible Behaviors**
	1. 2.	1. 2.	1. 2.

Day 6: _____

Situation	Original Thoughts	Original Feelings	Original Behaviors
	1. 2.	1. 2.	1. 2.
	Alternative Thoughts	**Possible Feelings**	**Possible Behaviors**
	1. 2.	1. 2.	1. 2.

Day 7: _____

Situation	Original Thoughts	Original Feelings	Original Behaviors
	1. 2.	1. 2.	1. 2.
	Alternative Thoughts	**Possible Feelings**	**Possible Behaviors**
	1. 2.	1. 2.	1. 2.

At the end of the week, respond to the following questions:

What thoughts were you able to challenge successfully by coming up with an alternative thought?

_____

_____

What thoughts were you **NOT** able to challenge successfully?

_____

_____

How did your thoughts impact your feelings?

_____

_____

How did your thoughts and feelings impact your behavior?

_____

_____

What is one situation from this week when you could have responded differently based on using your "alternative thoughts"?

_____

_____

What is a situation in which you were able to _effectively_ challenge your thoughts, come up with an alternative, and make a different choice? Was the choice more helpful or adaptive?

_____

_____

How do you think the situation might have been different if you had not changed your thoughts?

_____

_____

3

THE BODY'S RESPONSE TO TRAUMA

One core tenant of the impact of trauma on children and adolescents is the idea that there is a reciprocal relationship between trauma and development. In particular, an individual's development *prior* to a trauma influences their individual reactions to that experience. At the same time, the experience of that trauma – combined with the aftermath of changes in the individual's environment that often *follow* trauma – can have a significant impact on an individual's development post-trauma (NCTSN, 2012). For example, an adolescent who has experienced domestic violence in their home at an early age may be more susceptible to having a traumatic response to a car accident than a teen whose early home life was characterized by safe, warm, and supportive relationships. In the aftermath of the car accident and the resulting trauma that it caused, the teen is more likely to be attuned to possible threats in her environment, which may result in behavioral changes that limit her ability to continue the normal developmental tasks of adolescence. For example, if after experiencing the car accident, she refuses to leave the house out of fear of a future automobile accident, then her ability to engage in age-appropriate social, educational, and recreational activities will be severely limited.

While a comprehensive review of the neurobiology of stress and trauma is beyond the scope of this workbook, some basic understanding of the influence of trauma on the adolescent's physiology is needed in order to effectively provide trauma treatment. The human body's physiological response to stress includes a systemic response that impacts many aspects of the body's physiology. As we discussed in Chapter 2, the brain and nervous system respond in specific ways to trauma, but the circulatory system, digestive system, hormones, and even immune system are also impacted. These changes that accompany the stress response are protective, in that they prepare the individual to survive a dangerous situation. This response is often referred to as the **fight, flight, or freeze response**. The symptoms that accompany this response, such as rapid breathing or pounding heart, are adaptive in the context of danger or threat because they mobilize the body to take action.

Importantly, the experience of trauma, compared to short-term stressors, can lead to more longstanding changes to these body systems. These long-term changes can be understood as the body's way of anticipating danger in the future. That is, the body becomes "fine-tuned" to respond to potentially stressful or threatening situations. These changes are adaptive in the sense that the body becomes primed to activate the fight, flight, or freeze response more quickly in dangerous situations, which improve the individual's chances for survival.

On the other hand, these changes can also lead to activation of the stress response in situations that are stressful, but not actually life-threatening. For example, a teen who has been exposed to physical and verbal abuse may appear to "overreact" when a teacher raises his or her voice in class. In this case, the teacher's raised voice, while perceived by other students simply as loud or stern, may be interpreted as threatening by an adolescent who has previously associated loud voices with physical and emotional threat. When the body's physiological response system becomes hypersensitive in this manner, the fight, flight, or freeze response is in a state of constant overactivation. This overactivation, in turn, can result in the symptoms of hypervigilance and hyperarousal associated with PTSD. In adolescents, this hypervigilance and hyperarousal may present as restlessness, inattention, or a constant need to know what everyone around them is doing at all times.

In addition to the symptoms of hyperarousal commonly associated with PTSD, adolescents who have experienced trauma may also exhibit other physical symptoms. For example, they may be under- or over-responsive to sensory stimuli. Heightened sensitivity to loud noises, bright lights, and large crowds are typical ways in which many adolescents display symptoms of hypersensitivity. **Adolescents who are hyposensitive may exhibit sensation-seeking behaviors, such as driving fast, using substances, or engaging in self-injury (e.g., cutting).** Alternatively, teens might present with somatic symptoms, such as frequent and unexplained stomachaches or headaches. Left untreated, these longer-term changes to the body's physiology can follow adolescents into adulthood and result in the development of several health risks, including heart disease, cancer, and even premature death (Felitti et al., 1998).

HOW TO INCORPORATE WORKSHEETS ON THE BODY'S RESPONSE TO TRAUMA

The exercises in this section are focused on helping adolescents increase their understanding of their own brain and body. This chapter provides worksheets to introduce teens to the basic physiological concepts of the body's stress response, as well as explain the fight, flight, or freeze response that frequently accompanies traumatic events. Activities are provided to help teens increase their awareness of the stress and trauma responses in their own body. Increased understanding about the body's response to stress and trauma can help to demystify and normalize the teen's trauma symptoms. Additionally, building on the basic cognitive skills discussed in Chapter 2, the worksheets in this section can help adolescents reframe their symptoms as self-protective – as signs of strength and resilience, rather than personal problems, deficits, or weaknesses.

Adolescents will also increase their language for describing the ways in which their body responds to triggers, with special attention paid to the ways in which the body stores memories – not just verbally, but through all five senses. Specific activities are included to help teens understand the concept of sensory memories, to explore the specific sensory memories related to their trauma, and to finally make the link between specific sensory triggers and trauma responses in their own body. These activities expand on the basic concept of triggers presented in Chapter 1 by adding concepts of the physiological stress response and sensory memory.

Finally, there are activities in this section that help the teen identify the ways in which trauma is linked to physical sensations in their body. The focus of these activities is twofold: to normalize the body's physiological response to trauma triggers and to provide an opportunity for gradual exposure to trauma-related triggers. Gradual exposure – in the context of a supportive therapeutic relationship and combined with concrete tools for identifying, labeling, and managing distress as it arises – is an important element of trauma treatment.

LEARNING ABOUT STRESS

· · · · · ·

What is Stress?

There are several different ways to define stress. At the most basic level, it is how you respond when you must adapt or react to a change or challenging situation.

How Does Stress Affect Your Body?

Your body reacts in many different ways under stress. Look at the following list, and circle all of the physical symptoms of stress that you have experienced.

Stomachache	Cold hands or feet	Loss of appetite
Headache	Rapid breathing	Dizziness
Feeling tired	Sweating	Stiff neck or shoulders
Heart pounding	Trouble sleeping	Back pain

How Does Stress Affect Your Feelings?

People may experience a variety of different feelings when they are stressed. Look at the following list, and circle any words that describe how stress feels for you.

Anxiety	Sad or depressed	Pessimism
Anger	Overwhelmed	Irritable
Mood swings	Racing thoughts	Nightmares
Panic attacks	Confusion	Difficulty concentrating

How Does Stress Affect Your Behaviors?

When people are stressed, they may behave in lots of different ways. Look at the following list, and circle any behaviors that you have done when you have been stressed.

Fidgeting	Sleeping too much	Nail biting
Skipping school	Avoiding others	Eating too much/little
Using drugs or alcohol	Disorganization	Procrastination

FLIPPING STRESS UPSIDE DOWN

• • • • • •

Most people think that stress is a bad thing and something that you should always try to avoid. These people are missing something very important, and that is the fact that **stress is your body's natural way of helping you to deal with the situation or change**. Stress helps you to know when a situation is important and gives you the energy and motivation to do something about it.

When you notice your heart pounding, your muscles tightening, and your hands sweating, those are all ways that **your body is giving you the energy and resources that you need** to get through the stressful situation. For example, if you step into a crosswalk just as a car comes speeding around the corner in your direction, your body will respond with an immediate burst of energy that will allow you to quickly jump out of the path of danger.

The stress response **also lets you know which situations are important** to you, since you are not likely to feel stressed out if it is something that doesn't matter to you. For example, you are much more likely to feel stressed if your best friend tells you that he or she is moving out of town than if your neighbors (who you don't know very well) announce that they are moving away.

What's more, **the situations that cause you stress are also the situations from which you can learn the most**! Every time you encounter a stressful situation, you are increasing your skills to manage stress. Since stressful situations will always arise, these valuable skills will be helpful to you for the rest of your life.

In this exercise, you will be challenged to think of a situation that causes you stress and turn the stress upside down.

1. A situation that causes you stress is:

_____

_____

_____

2. How does your body react in this situation? What physical signs alert you that you are stressed?

_____

_____

_____

3. Now, think about how helpful it is that your body is letting you know that this is important enough for you to feel stressed about. Remind yourself that each of these warning signs in your body are your body's way of preparing you to face the challenge of the situation. What can you say to yourself to remember the positive aspects of stress?

_____

_____

_____

4. Ask yourself: What skill can I learn from surviving this stressful situation? After this is over, how might I be better prepared to face similar stressors in the future?

_____

_____

_____

Finally, give yourself a pat on the back for turning your stress upside down!
You have turned a stressful situation into a chance to learn and grow.
Congratulations!

FIGHT, FLIGHT, OR FREEZE RESPONSE

· · · · · · ·

Your body has a built-in system for managing dangerous situations, which is sometimes called the "fight-or-flight" response (or the fight, flight, or freeze response). Imagine for a moment that you are a cave person living thousands of years ago. You are walking at night through a dark forest. All of a sudden, you hear a loud noise behind you. What do you think it might be?

Well, it could be a lot of things. It could be a tree branch that has fallen from the wind. It could be the crack of thunder from an approaching rain storm. Or, perhaps, it could be a large and hungry animal, like a bear or a lion, about to attack.

Humans, like most animals, have evolved to survive. Therefore, your body is primed to react to that loud noise as if it were the worst-case scenario possible. Your heart will start to race, your muscles will become energized, and your breathing will become more rapid. All of these changes in your body will prepare you to fight back or flee the situation.

Signs of the fight, flight, or freeze response:

- Increased heart rate
- Racing thoughts
- Difficulty concentrating
- Dizziness or lightheadedness
- Nausea or "butterflies" in the stomach
- Rapid breathing
- Shaking
- Sweating
- Tense muscles

As you may have noticed in your own life, ***the fight-or-flight response is very strong and can be very useful***, especially in life-threatening situations. If you have ever stepped out into the street only to realize at the last second that there is a car racing towards you, you may have noticed how useful your body's fight-or-flight response can be!

Unfortunately, while the fight-or-flight response is strong, it is not very specific. ***That means that this response can be triggered whenever you perceive danger, even if that danger is not life-threatening at all***. Think for a moment about a time when you felt very embarrassed. How did your body respond? That was most likely your fight-or-flight response kicking in!

In the case where fighting back and running away are not possible, ***you also have a third built-in response, which is to freeze***. Deer and rabbits often use this strategy in an effort to evade their predators: If they remain still in the face of danger, then there is a chance that they will go unnoticed and, in turn, survive the situation. In the case of a school shooting, for example, the instinct to hide and remain still and quiet may very well prove to be the safest possible choice.

Learning to understand and respond to your body's fight, flight, or freeze response is an important skill that can help you to feel more in control of your body, your feelings, and your behaviors.

FIGHT, FLIGHT, OR FREEZE?

. . . . . .

While every human has the built-in physiological fight-or-flight response, we each have our own personality and life experiences that influence how we respond to specific situations.

In some situations, we may tend to have a **fight response**. This may take the form of physical aggression, verbal arguments, or even just the impulse to blame the other person before they can blame you.

Other times, we may be more inclined to have a **flight response**. In addition to literally running away or leaving a situation, the flight response could include avoiding any situation that may cause stress and attempting to ignore or pretend that something is not happening so we don't have to deal with it.

Freeze responses are those times when we tend to shut down in the face of stress. This may take the form of being unable to speak or becoming frozen in place when certain situations arise.

For each of the following situations, check the box to indicate how you usually respond to that type of stressor (fight, flight, or freeze).

Check the box for the response you are most likely to have in the following situations:	Fight	Flight	Freeze
Being criticized or told you are doing something wrong			
Seeing someone fighting			
Being bumped into from behind			
Hearing yelling or screaming			
Being told what to do			
Being blamed for something you didn't do			
Making a mistake			
Having someone get in your personal space			
Hearing someone make unkind comments about or to you			
Being yelled at			
Feeling embarrassed			

TRAUMA IN MY BODY

· · · · · ·

When memories of trauma are triggered, it may feel as if your body is being hijacked. It is not uncommon for the feelings to be very intense, and you may even have difficulty recognizing what is happening until later (if ever). Learning to recognize your body's fight, flight, or freeze response is an important skill that can help you to feel more in control of your body, your feelings, and your behaviors.

Using the figures on the next page, indicate where in your body you feel the fight, flight, or freeze response. Remember, signs of this stress response include:

- Increased heart rate
- Racing thoughts
- Difficulty concentrating
- Dizziness or lightheadedness
- Nausea or "butterflies" in the stomach
- Rapid breathing
- Shaking
- Sweating
- Tense muscles

TRAUMA IN MY BODY DIAGRAM

· · · · · · ·

FRONT

BACK

75

SENSORY MEMORIES

. . . . . .

The body has many ways of encoding memories. One way is with words: These are the memories that can be told just like a story in that they have a beginning, middle, and an end. However, your brain can also store memories that are based primarily in pictures, sounds, smells, tastes, or physical feelings in your body. For example, the smell of your grandmother's favorite perfume may make you feel warm and calm, or the sound of kids playing baseball may bring up feelings of excitement and happiness. These are sometimes called **sensory memories**.

We all have sensory memories that include sights, sounds, tastes, smells, and physical feelings in our bodies.

In this exercise, you will practice identifying sensory memories by writing down sensory memories that are positive for you.

A smell that I love is

_____

_____

Whenever I hear

_____

_____

it reminds me of a really fun time in my life.

My favorite food tastes like

_____

_____

When I am happy, I feel

_____

_____

in my body.

_____

_____

makes me feel cozy and comforted.

SENSORY DETECTIVE

• • • • • •

When you are in a stressful or traumatic situation, your brain switches into self-protective mode. When you are in this self-protective mode, you are less likely to store memories in word-based stories and may be more likely to form sensory memories.

For this activity, you will think about one difficult, stressful, or traumatic situation that you have experienced in your life. Once you have identified the situation, you are going to act like a detective. See how many sensory aspects of the situation you can remember. You do not need to report on what happened in the situation. Rather, focus only on reporting the specific sensations (sight, hearing, smell, touch, taste) that went along with the memory.

On the next page, write down as many different sensations associated with the memory as you can recall, and make sure to include specific details. You want to be as specific as you can. If someone were to read this, you want them to be able to picture the setting in their mind as accurately as possible.

If you are having trouble remembering the sensations associated with the memory, you can close your eyes and briefly imagine that you are watching yourself when the event happened.

Remembering traumatic events is difficult. If you start to feel anxious or afraid, you can open your eyes at any time. By focusing on each of the sensations separately, you may feel more in control of your memories.

What I **saw**:

_____

_____

_____

What I **smelled**:

_____

_____

_____

What I **tasted**:

_____

_____

_____

What I **heard**:

_____

_____

_____

What I **felt** in my body:

_____

_____

_____

Being aware of the sensory memories related to your trauma will help you to understand your trauma triggers and be better prepared to manage those triggers.

In addition, each time you allow yourself to remember part of the trauma without getting overwhelmed by the memory, you are building your skills for managing the memories and feelings. Just like building muscles takes practice and lots of repetition, so does the skill of managing trauma reminders.

TRAUMA TRIGGERS

· · · · · ·

Trauma triggers are those situations, people, places, thoughts, and feelings that trigger memories of past traumatic events. When trauma memories are triggered, you may experience strong feelings in your body and even flashbacks, where you feel as if you are back at the time of the trauma, living it all over again.

One way to deal with trauma triggers is to **avoid or reduce exposure** to the triggers. Avoidance can *sometimes* be a good option when the triggers to trauma are very specific. For example, you might find it useful to avoid a specific location where a trauma occurred (when it is not a location that you are required to be in, such as your home or school) or to avoid a person who was responsible for the trauma.

However, there are other times when you will not be able to avoid the triggers or when avoiding the triggers may have a negative impact on your life. For example, if you were traumatized by a car accident, your life may be significantly limited if you were to decide to stop riding in cars. In these cases, you will need to develop **strategies for managing your triggers**.

Here are a few things to remember about managing trauma triggers:

1. Being aware of your triggers will help you prepare.

2. Making a plan ahead of time will increase the likelihood that you can successfully manage the triggers when they arise.

3. Coping strategies are more likely to work if you have practiced them before, so practice them before you need them.

The first step in managing your triggers is to identify *what* your trauma triggers are. Therefore, in order to help you develop a trauma trigger plan, first write down all of the triggers (sight, hearing, smell, touch, taste) that you can think of:

Things that I **see** that trigger me:

_____

_____

_____

Smells that are triggering:

_____

_____

_____

Sounds that are triggering:

_____

_____

_____

I am triggered by the following **physical feelings** in my body:

_____

_____

_____

Emotions that trigger me:

_____

_____

_____

Situations that are triggering:

_____

_____

_____

These **places** are triggers for me:

_____

_____

_____

MY TRAUMA TRIGGER PLAN

· · · · · ·

Now that you have identified several of your trauma triggers, pick three or four triggers that bother you the most. **Use the form below to develop a trauma trigger plan**. Once you have your plan in place, commit to implementing the plan for one week.

Trigger #1:	Is this a trigger I can avoid or reduce? If so, how?
	What coping strategies can I use to manage this trigger when I can't avoid it?
Trigger #2:	Is this a trigger I can avoid or reduce? If so, how?
	What coping strategies can I use to manage this trigger when I can't avoid it?
Trigger #3:	Is this a trigger I can avoid or reduce? If so, how?
	What coping strategies can I use to manage this trigger when I can't avoid it?
Trigger #4:	Is this a trigger I can avoid or reduce? If so, how?
	What coping strategies can I use to manage this trigger when I can't avoid it?

TRAUMA TRIGGER PLAN REFLECTION

. . . . . .

After implementing your trauma trigger plan for one week, answer the following questions by circling the number that best corresponds with your response:

1. I used my trauma trigger plan:

    1 – Never

    2 – Rarely

    3 – Sometimes

    4 – Often

    5 – Always

2. Using my trauma trigger plan was:

    1 – Very difficult

    2 – Difficult

    3 – Neutral

    4 – Easy

    5 – Very easy

3. After using my trauma trigger plan for one week, I feel:

    1 – Much worse

    2 – Somewhat worse

    3 – About the same

    4 – Somewhat better

    5 – Much better

Total score = _____

*Note your total score for these three questions. If it is not as high as you would like it to be, try this activity again and see if your score increases.

SELF-REGULATION SKILLS

$\mathbb{S}$ elf-regulation refers to our ability to monitor and control our own behavior and our emotions, as well as our ability to act based on what is best for our long-term interests. In particular, it involves the ability to tolerate and manage a wide variety of strong emotions, to resist the urge to engage in impulsive behaviors, to modulate responses to a variety of situations, and to pursue long-term goals. For example, consider a teen who is feeling stressed out because of school and some recent interpersonal conflict with his peers. He comes home from a long day, only to hear his parent say, "Why haven't you done your chores yet?" In this situation, being able to self-regulate involves the ability to take a calming breath before answering, rather than yelling at his parent and storming out of the room.

However, individuals who experience trauma frequently experience impairments in self-regulation, which can result in symptoms such as persistent negative feelings, intrusive thoughts and memories about the trauma, difficulty experiencing positive emotions, and irritability in the aftermath of trauma. Teenagers who have experienced trauma may find that they more frequently feel vulnerable, experience hypervigilance (with regard to issues of safety at home, school, and in the community), and are more likely to interpret situations as negative or threatening (Perry, Pollard, Blakley, Baker, & Vigilante, 1995). These symptoms may manifest as a change in friendships (e.g., not spending time with peers that were previously frequent companions) or increased irritability and negativity towards teachers (e.g., due to feelings that the teacher is unfairly targeting them or does not understand them). Similar reactions in teen-parent interactions may also occur, with the adolescent expressing a sense of being increasingly criticized or treated poorly. Teens may also withdraw from family or social events, and they may exhibit reduced awareness of their emotions or thoughts, which is a form of emotional dissociation that can make it difficult for teens to understand, express, or modulate their behaviors (Foa & Hearst-Ikeda, 1996).

Interventions to build self-regulation skills can focus on either the thoughts driving the behaviors or the feelings underlying the behaviors. These interventions are often referred to as *top-down* versus *bottom-up* approaches, respectively. Both can be effective and important strategies, depending on the individual and the specific situation. For instance, if a situation is only mildly arousing, then using a top-down approach to address the cognitions surrounding the event can be helpful. As an example, consider a teen who gets a paper back in class and immediately begins to feel upset upon seeing that there are a lot of comments and red ink on the paper. In turn, the teenager starts to crumple up the paper. This is a situation in which the teen's thoughts ("Oh no, I failed") are driving the behavior (e.g., increased tension, crumpling the paper). In this situation, the teen can engage in top-down regulation by reminding him or herself, "I need to see what the comments are first if I want to improve next time."

However, it is important to keep in mind that when the body's physiological trauma response is activated, the higher order functions of the brain – which control cognitive reasoning – are impaired. Therefore, it is often necessary to first help teenagers use bottom-up approaches to physiologically regulate their body before attempting to utilize cognitive strategies. The **first level of intervention** is always to decrease arousal so that adolescents can access and utilize their pre-frontal cortex, which is the area of the brain that governs cognitive control. Breathing strategies are the most effective tools to decrease arousal, which can also be supplemented by other sensory techniques, such as visualization of a calming scene, use of a music playlist that enhances calming, or specific essential oils or scents that the teen associates with calm (all of which are included in the worksheets for this chapter).

In addition, enhancing self-regulation skills can be beneficial not only to adolescents who have been impacted by traumatic events, but to their parents as well. Parents of teens in treatment may especially benefit from learning these strategies alongside their child. When a parent is able to utilize self-regulation skills in the context of challenging interactions with their teens, they are both role-modeling a skill that is vital to interpersonal success and coping, and also decreasing the potential for escalation of differences within the parent-child dyad.

HOW TO INCORPORATE THE SELF-REGULATION SKILLS WORKSHEETS

This section includes worksheets to assist the therapist in teaching teen patients a variety of self-regulation skills, including stress management, physiological soothing, emotion regulation, and cognitive regulation. Stress management strategies are often a good place to start when working on the development of self-regulation skills with teenagers. When introducing this concept with teens, it can be helpful to emphasize that individuals (regardless of whether they have experienced trauma) can benefit from having a wide variety of stress management strategies that they can call upon in different situations. One reason for this is that the demands of different situations can vary (e.g., what may be allowed at home on the weekend, such as listening to a favorite song, may not be allowed or accessible during math class at school), so having a toolbox full of stress management strategies is always helpful. It is also important to acknowledge that the effectiveness of these strategies can vary from individual to individual, and some strategies may become less effective across time with repeated use.

Although stress management strategies are a great way to initially introduce self-regulation skills to teenagers, they should not be used in isolation. As treatment progresses, the therapist should be especially mindful to ensure that these techniques do not begin to drive excessive avoidance behaviors, which is extremely common after trauma. In this respect, it is important to also introduce other strategies that are included in this section, such as body-based regulation (physiological soothing), changing self-talk, and time management skills. Changing self-talk is a means for the adolescent to begin to treat themselves with greater care and compassion, which can allow for an increased ability to tolerate challenging emotions. Time management skills are an effective means of addressing potential stressors before they occur, supporting the adolescent in being able to feel a greater sense of agency, rather than feeling overwhelmed. In addition, the skills introduced in Chapters 5 (increasing positive feelings) and Chapter 7 (making meaning after trauma) can be used to help teens find a healthy balance between distraction, staying present in the moment, and acknowledging their feelings.

When introducing the exercises on physiological soothing, it is important to remember that individuals who have experienced trauma often struggle initially to practice physiological soothing activities, such as deep breathing and relaxation. In fact, many adolescents who have experienced trauma will even report that they do not want to feel relaxed because it feels too vulnerable or unsafe. In these cases, teens can benefit from understanding not only the rationale behind these skills, but also from being provided with reassurance that using these skills will *in no way* impair their adaptive physiological response to real threats in their environment. Rather, the goal of these skills is to recalibrate their fear response so that this reaction is triggered only in situations that are actually dangerous, rather than being triggered in everyday, non-threatening situations.

In addition to physiological strategies for self-regulation, cognitive strategies also provide a helpful framework for altering thoughts and behaviors. As discussed in Chapter 2, teenagers who have experienced trauma frequently experience thinking errors, particularly in terms of polarized thought processes ("black and white thinking") and overestimating potential negative outcomes ("catastrophizing"). Learning to identify the various thinking errors and developing new cognitive frameworks allows teenagers to better down-regulate (e.g., reduce the intensity of) their emotional response.

USING COPING STRATEGIES

· · · · · · ·

Stress is something that is part of everyone's life. However, when we are feeling "stressed," it can be hard to concentrate, feel positive, or take action. Sometimes, when we feel really stressed, we tend to do even less (which actually increases the feeling of stress). Although there are several active, healthy coping tools that we can use to deal with stress, we sometimes also use avoidance as a way of coping. Even though avoidance may feel like a good idea in the moment, it doesn't help us address the stress in a way that will help us move forward. **This worksheet will help you to think about stress and figure out healthy coping skills**.

1. What are some things that cause you stress?

_____

_____

_____

2. What do you usually do when you are feeling stressed?

_____

_____

_____

3. What is *helpful* about the choices you usually make when you are stressed?

_____

_____

_____

4. What is *difficult or problematic* about the choices you usually make when you are stressed?

_____

_____

_____

5. What are three things you WISH you could do instead?

_____

_____

_____

6. How would making a choice to do something different help you?

_____

_____

_____

7. How might making a choice to do something different cause a problem?

_____

_____

_____

8. Look at the list of "Healthy vs. Unhealthy Coping Strategies" page 88, and list any strategies you have used in the past two weeks.

_____

_____

_____

9. What are two ideas of healthy coping strategies from the list (that you haven't tried yet) that you *might* be willing to try?

_____

_____

_____

10. What are two new ideas (not on the list of "Healthy and Unhealthy Coping Strategies") that you *might* be willing to try?

_____

_____

_____

11. Who is someone you trust that can help you brainstorm new options?

_____

_____

_____

12. What's one healthy coping strategy that you are willing to try during the next week?

_____

_____

_____

HEALTHY VS. UNHEALTHY COPING STRATEGIES

· · · · · ·

Unhealthy Coping Strategies

- Procrastination
- Alcohol use
- Drug use
- Overeating
- Physical aggression
- Self-harm
- Picking a fight (either verbal or physical)
- Exercising too much
- Sleeping too much
- Staying away from friends
- Not engaging in regular activities

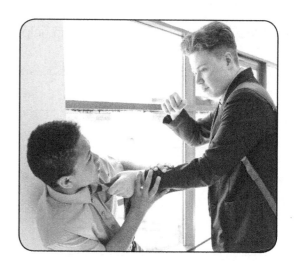

Healthy Coping Strategies

- Talking to a friend
- Talking to a trusted adult
- Spending time with friends
- Doing activities with your family
- Exercise
- Relaxation
- Eating healthily
- Working with a therapist
- Writing in a journal
- Doing something creative
- Using a problem-solving strategy
- Playing with a pet

COPING STRATEGY PLANNING

· · · · · ·

Planning for what might be stressful and how to handle the situation is a great way to get into the habit of using healthy coping skills. **Let's use some examples from your life to identify what strategies you've been using and see how well they are working.**

SITUATION

In as much detail as possible, describe a situation that is currently bothering you or that makes you feel anxious.

_____

_____

_____

_____

_____

_____

_____

WHAT I USUALLY DO

1. Unhealthy coping strategy: _____
   Consequence of using this strategy: _____
2. Unhealthy coping strategy: _____
   Consequence of using this strategy: _____

TRY SOMETHING DIFFERENT

1. Healthy coping strategy: _____
   Potential outcome from using this strategy: _____
2. Barriers to using this strategy: _____
   _____
3. What can you do to overcome any barriers you've identified? (If you're feeling stuck, you may want to brainstorm ideas with someone else to do this exercise) _____
   _____
   _____

HEALTHY COPING ACTIVITIES

• • • • • •

The following list contains additional healthy coping activities that you can use for managing stress. It's often helpful to have a list of potential activities planned out ahead of time. That way, if you can't think of a strategy in the moment, you can just look at the list. It can also be helpful to pick activities that you don't usually do, or that you may have done when you were younger. For example, kids, teens, and adults can all enjoy blowing bubbles and trying to see how big of a bubble they can make.

- Doodle
- Color a mandala
- Draw a picture
- Paint your feelings
- Draw a self-portrait
- Make a chalk drawing
- Make playdough
- Do origami
- Make a puppet
- Create a puppet show
- Create a journal
- Write in your journal
- Write a gratitude letter
- Write a story
- Write a poem or haiku
- List every food you like
- Take photographs
- Make a photo album
- Create a happy playlist
- Make a video

- Play with marbles
- Blow bubbles
- Build something with Legos®
- Take a walk outside
- Find different colored leaves
- Find a cool stone
- Paint your stone
- Create a memory jar
- Watch the clouds
- Listen to the birds
- Play hopscotch
- Jump rope
- Use clay and make a bowl
- Paint your nails
- Try a new hairstyle
- Go for a run
- Plan a scavenger hunt
- Sew
- Have a picnic
- Sing

- Make cookies
- Find a recipe for a new meal
- Make ice cream
- Make a blanket fort
- Organize your closet
- Find clothes to donate
- Cuddle up with a blanket
- Use essential oils
- Hug a stuffed animal
- Talk to a friend
- Play a board game
- Play checkers or chess
- Practice deep breathing
- Exercise
- Do pushups
- Practice yoga
- Count the stars
- Plant flowers
- Create a fairy garden
- Clean your room
- Wish on the moon
- Vacuum or dust
- Tie-dye a shirt
- Pet a dog or cat
- Light a candle
- Hug a friend
- Crochet or knit
- Play a computer game
- Play in the water
- Practice meditation
- Ride a bike
- Walk a dog
- Balance on one leg

LEARNING TO BREATHE

Explain to your clients that when they are anxious, stressed, angry, or sad, their breathing may be quick and/or shallow. Breathing in this manner does not allow enough oxygen to reach their organs, and it can cause them to hyperventilate.

When this happens, it can feel as if they can't catch their breath. The more worried or upset they become, the harder it is to breathe properly. This is because their internal stress alarm is going off. In order to reduce the volume and intensity of this "alarm" system, it can be very helpful to practice deep breathing techniques.

Clients should start practicing these techniques as soon as they notice that they are starting to feel uncomfortable or distressed, as opposed to waiting until the anxiety feels too overwhelming.

BREATHING TECHNIQUE #1: 4-7-8 BREATH

• • • • • •

Sit comfortably on a chair or the floor. Keep your back straight and allow your hands to rest in your lap or on your thighs.

Look ahead and slightly down (keeping your head straight). Try not to look at anything in particular. You can also close your eyes if this is comfortable for you.

Begin to focus on your breathing, inhaling through your NOSE and exhaling through your MOUTH.

Let the tip of your tongue touch the top of your mouth, just behind your top teeth.

Begin to inhale slowly, while counting to 4 seconds. Fill your lower lungs first (by pushing out your belly), then your middle and upper lungs.

Hold your breath for a mental count of 7 seconds.

Slowly exhale your breath for a count of 8 seconds. While you are exhaling, imagine letting go of all your anxiety, tension, and stress.

That's one round. Pause briefly without inhaling for 2 seconds, and then start another round. Try doing 10-12 rounds to begin. With practice, you should build up to doing 25-30 rounds several times a day AND whenever you feel anxious, stressed, nervous, etc.

Summary: Inhale for 4 seconds - Hold for 7 seconds - Exhale for 8 seconds - Pause briefly - Repeat.

BREATHING TECHNIQUE #2: ALTERNATE NOSTRIL BREATH (NADI SHODHANA)

· · · · · ·

Sit comfortably on a chair or the floor. Keep your back straight and allow your hands to rest in your lap or on your thighs.

Close the right nostril with your right thumb and inhale slowly through the left nostril.

Close the left nostril with your right ring finger, remove your thumb from the right nostril, and exhale slowly through the right nostril.

Then, inhale through the right nostril, close the right nostril with your right thumb, and exhale through the left nostril.

Repeat this sequence of breath three or four times.

Remember that with this technique, you are inhaling and exhaling only through your NOSE.

Summary: Inhale on the left, exhale on the right. Inhale on the right, exhale on the left.

BREATHING TECHNIQUE #3:
BASIC DEEP BELLY BREATH

• • • • • •

Breathe in through your nose and pay attention to the rise in your lower abdomen.

Breathe out through your mouth noisily and let your lower abdomen fall.

Breathe in through your nose as your middle abdomen rises.

Breathe out through your mouth noisily and let your middle abdomen fall.

Breathe in as your upper abdomen rises. Now "force" the oxygen into the extremities of your body, such as your hands, feet, and skull. Feel it spreading through your bloodstream to these parts.

Breathe out noisily as your abdomen falls.

Summary: As you breathe in through your nose and out through your mouth, watch your belly rise and fall. Belly rises on the inhale and falls on the exhale.

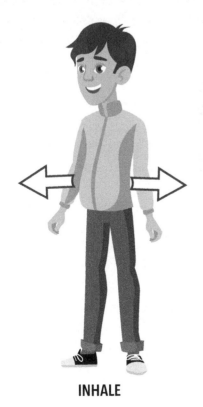

INHALE

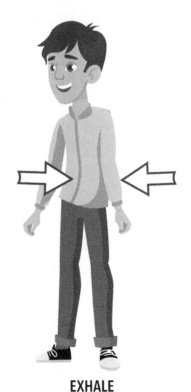

EXHALE

BREATHING TECHNIQUE #4: SQUARE BREATHING (TACTICAL BREATHING)

· · · · · ·

Inhale through your nose for a count of 4, making sure to start your breath deep within your belly and pushing your belly out.

Hold your breath for a count of 4.

Exhale through your nose for a count of 4, allowing your chest and belly to fall in. Hold for a count of 4.

Repeat 3 times.

You can also try drawing a square with your finger (on a desk or on your palm) while breathing to stay on track.

Summary: Breathe in for 4, hold for 4, breathe out for 4, hold for 4. Belly rises on the inhale and falls on the exhale.

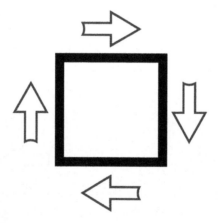

PROGRESSIVE MUSCLE RELAXATION

· · · · · ·

Learning to relax the different parts of your body is a great way to reduce stress, and it is also helpful if you are having a hard time going to sleep. **Progressive muscle relaxation is one technique that you can use, which involves tensing the muscles in one part of your body while you breathe in, and then relaxing those same muscles as you breathe out**. This lets you relax each area of your body (and also helps to relax your mind). You do each area of the body once and then typically repeat the whole process, though you can also do each area 2-3 times as you go through the parts of the body. Some people find it easier to do this exercise lying down, but you can also do this while sitting or even standing.

Start by taking two deep breaths, inhaling through your nose and exhaling through your mouth (so you can hear yourself sighing).

Pay attention to the muscles in your face. Relax them, beginning with your jaw. Then, clench your teeth for a couple of seconds and then let go. Next, scrunch up your nose super tightly, making lots of wrinkles in your face. Then, relax. Notice how relaxed your face feels when you let the tension go.

Next, push up your shoulders, trying to reach your ears. After a few seconds, let your shoulders relax and feel the tension melt away. Try to stretch your arms above your head and back as far is comfortable, then let your arms drop.

Squeeze the muscles in your right hand as hard as you can for about 3-5 seconds.

Pay attention to the tension in your muscles. Now, let your muscles relax. Repeat this for your left arm.

Squeeze your belly as hard as you can, holding this for 3-5 seconds. Then, let your belly relax. Do the same thing with your rear end, holding it firm and tight for 3-5 seconds, then letting it relax.

Squeeze your toes in, using the muscles in your legs to squeeze your toes as hard as you can. After a few seconds, relax your toes. Now tighten the muscles in your calves as hard as possible, then relax. Finally, squeeze the muscles in your thighs as hard as you can, holding for 3-5 seconds. Then, relax your legs.

Last, pretend you're a rag doll, and let your entire body relax.

USING COLOR

• • • • • •

Another technique to help relax your body involves using color imagery in tandem with the breath.

First, think of a color that you find relaxing or soothing. Some common colors that people find relaxing are green and blue. You can pick whatever color you want. Be creative – just make sure that you pick a color that represents calmness for you.

Close your eyes or lower your gaze. Take in two deep breaths, breathing in through your nose and out through your mouth. Sigh out loud if you can, letting all of the air exit from your body.

Return to your regular breathing. Keeping your eyes closed or your gaze lowered, envision the relaxing color that you identified earlier. Picture this color as clearly and brightly as you can.

As you breathe in, imagine that you are breathing in that color. As you continue breathing, allow the color to spread throughout your body. Let the color reach every place in your body, even your fingers and toes.

IMAGERY AND GUIDED IMAGERY

· · · · · ·

Imagery is another very powerful technique that our brains can use to help us get into a certain emotional or mental mindset. We can use imagery to help us feel calm, to feel confident, to improve at a sport or public speaking – and so many more ways!

Professional athletes and movie stars regularly use imagery to prepare for a big game or an audition. If we create a mental image that has strong enough sensory components – making sure to engage our sense of sight, smell, touch, taste, and hearing – our brain can't tell the difference between what we're imaging and the real thing.

One common reason that people use imagery is to feel safe or calm. First, think of a place that you associate with feeling safe and calm. If this is a real place that you have been to, that's great. Even if it's a place you've read about or just seen in a picture, that can work too.

Close your eyes and get comfortable. Take in a couple of deep breaths, sighing the breath out of your mouth.

Picture this safe and calm place as clearly as you can in your mind. Think of as many possible details as you can. What do you see? Try to notice the colors and anything else that is visible. For example, if you are imagining the beach, pay attention to the color of the sand and the color of the water, perhaps even noticing the little whitecaps on top of the waves.

Next, notice what you can smell as vividly as possible. If you are imagining that you are at the beach, this might be the smell of salt water, the smell of suntan lotion, or any other smells you associate with the beach.

Now, pay attention to what you hear. Maybe you hear seagulls or the sound of the waves gently crashing against the shoreline. Using your safe, calm image, add in as many aspects of hearing as you can.

Next, imagine what you can feel. What does the ground feel like beneath your feet? What is the temperature? Perhaps you feel the warmth of the sun or a cooling breeze.

Finally, add in whatever you can taste that you associate with this safe and calm place. Sometimes, there's a special food or drink that you associate with feeling calm, like warm tea or hot chocolate.

Imagine the whole scene, using as many of the sensory elements that you identified as possible. Keep breathing while you are imagining this place, and let the feelings of calm and safety flow through your body.

SENSORY MENU

· · · · · ·

One way to regulate your feelings is to engage your five senses: sight, taste, smell, sound, and touch. When you *purposely* seek to engage your senses, your body and your feelings begin a natural process of self-regulation.

The type of sensory input that works for you may be different than that which works for someone else. For example, some people find that they need sensory input that is calming in order to regulate their body, such as being in a dimly lit room (sight) with soft music (sound) and a cozy blanket (touch). Other people find that they need much stronger sensory input in order to self-regulate, such as sour tasting candy (taste), loud music (sound), or a firm stress ball (touch). You will know what type of sensory input works best for you because when you sense it, your body will react in a way that feels good to you.

In this activity, you will be creating a menu of sensory items that you find comforting, soothing, or that help you feel good. Just like a good restaurant menu has several selections for appetizers, entrees, drinks, and desserts, your sensory menu should have several options for each sensory category.

The following list includes some ideas to get you started, but don't feel limited by the ideas listed. Be as creative as possible in thinking of the sensations that you personally find most regulating.

Sight:
- Picture of a loved one, pet, family member, and/or friend
- LED light ball
- Pictures of a place you enjoy or would like to go
- Glitter jar
- Funny pictures
- Dark room
- Candlelight
- Blacklight or lava lamp

Sound:
- Favorite songs
- White noise
- Nature sounds
- Bells, chimes, or singing bowl

Taste:
- Sour candy
- Chocolate
- Hard candy or lollipop
- Mint
- Gum
- Crunchy snack
- Chewy candy
- Tea or hot cocoa

Touch:
- Clay, playdough, putty, or slime
- Fidget toy
- Worry stone
- Fuzzy or soft blanket
- Stress ball

Smell:
- Scented lotion
- Essential oils
- Flowers
- Candle
- Bottles of spices (like vanilla or cinnamon)
- Incense

MY SENSORY MENU

· · · · · ·

Sight:

Sound:

Taste:

Touch:

Smell:

USING SENSORY INPUT TO INTERRUPT
THE FIGHT-OR-FLIGHT RESPONSE

· · · · · ·

As you have learned, memories are stored both in your brain and in your body. You have also learned that your brain and body are continually sending messages back and forth in both directions.

By introducing sensory input of your choice, you can take advantage of the connections between your brain and body to change how you react and feel. This technique can be especially helpful when your body is experiencing the fight-or-flight response. **By intentionally introducing a sight, sound, smell, taste, touch, or other sensory input that is soothing to, you can interrupt the fight-or-flight process**.

Now that you have identified the sensory menu of tools that you prefer, let's think about how you might use those tools in certain situations. Use the following spaces to think about what sensory inputs would help you to interrupt the fight-or-flight response. Some of the sensory inputs you previously identified may not seem as easy to implement when you are feeling stressed, so it helps to plan this ahead of time.

Sights:	Sounds:
Tastes:	**Smells:**
Physical Touch:	**Other:**

USING SMELL TO CREATE RELAXATION

· · · · · ·

As human beings, our sense of smell is very strong. And as you have learned, our senses (and, in turn, our sensory memories) are directly connected to the limbic system and the amygdala. Given this, certain smells can often trigger certain emotional or even physical responses in us.

For example, driving by a field that is fertilized with cow manure may cause you to wrinkle your nose or hold your breath. Most of the time, we notice the smell of manure and find it somewhat distasteful. However, if you were raised on a farm and that was a smell that you associated with a productive harvest that supported your family, then you might not notice it at all or it might even jog a positive memory for you.

Similarly, we can find smells that help us feel relaxed, calm, secure, or joyful in the same way that we might identify other smells as negative or distasteful.

Essential oils are a good way to do this. Essential oils are typically natural scents, distilled from plants and flowers. The concentration of the smell is higher, so you can get a stronger response. Sometimes, people like to use scented candles, but typically the smell from the candle isn't as strong as if you were using an essential oil. **Try going to a natural foods store in your area and smelling different essential oils. Pick the one that most strongly supports the feeling you are wanting to enhance**.

As a general guide, **citrus smells** (lemon, orange, grapefruit) are often associated with energy, positivity, and happiness. Common stress reduction smells are **eucalyptus, rosemary, mint** and **peppermint**. Try **lavender** for better sleep.

POSTURE, MOVEMENT, AND MOOD

Explain to your teenage client that our nervous system is a two way street. Most people know that our brain is always sending messages to your body through the cells of the nervous system. But did your client know that our body is also always sending information back to our brain?

A simple example of this is our stomach. Our brain regulates when we get hungry and sends messages to our stomach to trigger digestive enzymes. Our stomach, in turn, sends messages back to let our brain know when it has been filled with food. Other parts of your body, including our muscles, are also continuously sending information back to our brain.

Scientists have recently begun to understand that memories and emotions are stored and processed throughout the entire body, not just in our brain. This means that we can use our body to help regulate our mood. When we change how our body is moving, in what way it moves, and even with what force it moves, we can trigger specific messages to be sent to our brain. These messages may ultimately help improve our mood.

On the following pages are a few simple activities your clients can try!

STANDING UP FOR YOURSELF

· · · · · ·

For this activity, you will be focusing on how you walk. You will practice walking with a straight back, your head held high, and your eyes looking straight ahead of you – making sure your gaze is up and forward. Make sure to hold your shoulders back, but not so much so that they are tense. Keep your arms hanging loosely at your sides, maybe swinging them slightly as you walk. Take each step purposely and confidently. This posture and style of walking has been shown to increase feelings of self-confidence and pride.

Practice walking like this for a whole day. At the end of the day, respond to these questions:

1. I practiced my posture and walk:

   1 – Never

   2 – Rarely

   3 – Sometimes

   4 – Often

   5 – Always

2. Practicing my posture and walk was:

   1 – Very difficult

   2 – Difficult

   3 – Neutral

   4 – Easy

   5 – Very easy

3. After practicing my posture and walk for one day, my confidence is:

   1 – Much worse

   2 – Somewhat worse

   3 – About the same

   4 – Somewhat better

   5 – Much better

Total score = _____

*Note your total score for these three questions. If it is not as high as you would like it to be, try this activity again and see if your score increases.

SUPERHERO POSE

· · · · · ·

The Superhero Pose

- Legs shoulder width apart
- Hands on hips
- Shoulders back
- Head held high

Believe it or not, research has shown that after standing in the superhero pose for just two minutes, people:

- Feel more powerful and confident
- Experience hormonal changes that decrease their experience of stress
- Act in more assertive ways

Stand like a superhero,

Feel like a superhero,

Act like a superhero.

SUPERHERO POSE REFLECTION

· · · · · ·

Practice your superhero pose for two minutes every morning for a week. Don't worry if you feel self-conscious or if it doesn't feel natural, and it is perfectly okay to do this practice in private. At the end of the week, respond to these questions:

1. I practiced the superhero pose:

    1 – Never

    2 – Rarely

    3 – Sometimes

    4 – Often

    5 – Always

2. Practicing the superhero pose was:

    1 – Very difficult

    2 – Difficult

    3 – Neutral

    4 – Easy

    5 – Very easy

3. After practicing the superhero pose for one week, my confidence is:

    1 – Much worse

    2 – Somewhat worse

    3 – About the same

    4 – Somewhat better

    5 – Much better

Total score = _____

*Note your total score for these three questions. If it is not as high as you would like it to be, try this activity again and see if your score increases.

PHYSICAL EXERCISE

· · · · · ·

You probably already know that physical exercise is good for your body. But did you know that exercise is also good for your mind? There's several ways exercise helps. For one, it causes your brain to release chemicals (endorphins) that make you feel good. It also increases cell growth (neurogenesis) in the brain, which helps you to learn better.

> **Mental Health Benefits of Physical Exercise:**
> Decreased symptoms of depression
> Decreased anxiety
> Increased feeling of calm
> Increased focus and attention
> Distraction from stressors
> Relaxation
> Increased motivation
> Increased energy
> Improved memory
> Increased self-esteem
> Better sleep
> Stronger resilience

What are your three favorite forms of exercise?

1. _____

2. _____

3. _____

MY EXERCISE PLAN

· · · · · ·

As you have learned, there are many physical and mental health benefits of regular exercise. This plan will help you to look at your current exercise habits and look at ways to increase your physical exercise.

1. Types of exercise I do regularly:

   _____

   _____

2. I usually exercise _____ days per week.

3. I usually exercise for _____ minutes.

4. I think I might like to try these types of exercise:

   _____

   _____

5. In addition to what we traditionally think of as "exercise," the following are simple ways that you can increase physical movement during your daily routines. Circle those that you are interested in trying.

   - Take the stairs instead of an elevator.
   - Walk while talking with a friend.
   - Stand instead of sitting.
   - Take stretch breaks when you are sitting for a long period of time.
   - Walk a longer route between your classes.
   - Dance, do squats, or walk in place while you are brushing your teeth.
   - Get off the bus one stop early and walk.
   - Wear a pedometer and aim for 10,000 steps per day.
   - Do sit-ups, push-ups, crunches, or jumping jacks during commercial breaks while watching TV.

Now that you have identified your current exercise habits, put a plan in place!

For the next two weeks, I commit to exercising _____ times per week for _____ minutes.

I commit to increasing my physical movement during my daily activities by:

_____

Use the chart on the following page to plan your exercise over the next two weeks and then record your actual exercise each day.

EXERCISE PLAN CHART

· · · · · ·

	SUN	MON	TUES	WED	THUR	FRI	SAT
Week 1 Plan:							
Week 1 Completed Exercise:							
Week 2 Plan:							
Week 2 Completed Exercise:							

EXERCISE PLAN REFLECTION

· · · · · ·

At the end of two weeks, answer these questions by circling the number that best corresponds with your response:

1. I increased my exercise:

1 – Never

2 – Rarely

3 – Sometimes

4 – Often

5 – Always

2. Increasing my exercise was:

1 – Very difficult

2 – Difficult

3 – Neutral

4 – Easy

5 – Very easy

3. After increasing my exercise for two weeks, I feel:

1 – Much worse

2 – Somewhat worse

3 – About the same

4 – Somewhat better

5 – Much better

Total score = _____

*Note your total score for these three questions. If it is not as high as you would like it to be, try this activity again and see if your score increases.

SAY "CHEESE"

· · · · · ·

Have you ever heard the phrase "fake it 'til you make it"? One situation in which this strategy is actually great advice is when you want to improve your mood. If you want to feel happier, one simple way to do it is to smile. Sounds too simple to be true, right?

Here's how it works: Normally, when you feel happy inside, your brain sends a message to your face to smile. What you might not realize is that your face is also sending messages *back* to your brain when you smile. Essentially, your face is telling your brain, "When I am in this position, it means that I am happy."

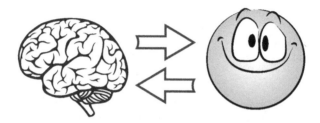

The same principles are true when you are unhappy. Your brain sends a message to your face to frown in order to express your unhappiness, and your face sends back messages to your brain reinforcing this unhappiness.

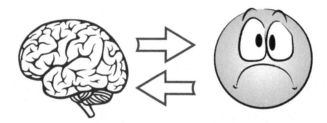

Things can happen in your environment or mind that will naturally shift you out of this happiness or unhappiness cycle. However, did you know that you can hijack this system by forcing yourself to smile more? It's true! When you force yourself to smile more, your brain starts to receive the message from your facial muscles telling your brain that you are happy. This process can interrupt the unhappiness cycle and start to lift your mood.

If this sounds too good to be true, that's okay! You can test it out for yourself. **Starting tomorrow, for one whole day, your assignment is to smile at everyone you meet**. You can also try to smile more even when you are alone.

SAY "CHEESE" REFLECTION

• • • • • •

At the end of the day, answer these questions:

1. I practiced smiling all day:

    1 – Not at all

    2 – A few times

    3 – Sometimes

    4 – Many times

    5 – Almost all the time

2. Practicing smiling was:

    1 – Very difficult

    2 – Difficult

    3 – Neutral

    4 – Easy

    5 – Very easy

3. After practicing smiling all day, I feel:

    1 – Much worse

    2 – Somewhat worse

    3 – About the same

    4 – Somewhat better

    5 – Much better

Total score = _____

*Note your total score for these three questions. If it is not as high as you would like it to be, try this activity again and see if your score increases.

THE SOOTHING POWER OF RHYTHM

· · · · · ·

Have you ever noticed that when people hold babies, they all tend to hold them in sort of the same way? They might gently rock them back and forth, or lightly pat the baby in a slow rhythm. People also tend to hold babies on their left side much more often than on their right side. Any idea why? Well, one reason seems to be that babies are soothed by hearing and feeling their caregiver's heartbeat.

So, that is all interesting and fine for babies, but what does it have to do with you? **Well, it turns out that rhythmic movements and sounds can be soothing for many people.** The neurobiology (brain) of a teen and an adult (and even animals) is the same as that of a baby. So, rhythmic movement helps! It's also true that our brains store all our sensory memories, including what we found to be soothing, as well as what may have been scary. Rhythmic movement that soothed you as a baby is still stored in your mind as a calming action, so it will still help you today (and as an adult).

Here are some ideas of rhythmic movements and sounds. Circle all of those which you find soothing.

Rocking chair	Swinging	Jumping on a trampoline
Tapping your foot	Ocean waves	Music with a steady beat
Listening to someone read	Drumming	Playing music
Dribbling a ball	Dancing	Singing

Can you think of any others?

_____

_____

GETTING ON THE BEAT

· · · · · ·

Music is a powerful tool that artists use to express their emotions. Listening to music can also be a great way to change the way that you are feeling. **Write down the names of songs that change your mood.**

Songs that calm or soothe me:

_____

_____

_____

Songs that energize me:

_____

_____

_____

Favorite songs to listen to with a friend or loved one:

_____

_____

Songs that make me happy:

_____

_____

_____

LEARNING ABOUT ANGER

· · · · · ·

Anger is a natural emotion. Every human being has had the experience of feeling angry at some point in their life – in fact, as young children, we feel anger frequently and often. Infants who are hungry and want to be fed, or who are uncomfortable and want to be changed, will loudly voice their displeasure. Young children act like this when their needs aren't immediately met because they don't yet have the capacity to understand how to make sense of what's happening.

Over time, we learn that we may have to wait for our needs to be met. Sometimes, though, no matter how long we wait, other people still can't meet our needs (or it isn't appropriate or possible for them to meet our needs). In these cases, our common response is to feel anger or frustration.

We also often experience anger when we feel that we are being misunderstood, treated unfairly, or when we feel threatened in some way. We may also experience anger when we are trying to cover up some other feeling, such as fear or sadness. Sometimes we aren't even aware of the feelings that are hiding underneath anger.

The first step in expressing our anger in an appropriate and helpful way involves acknowledging the feelings that we are experiencing, and then determining if there are other thoughts and feelings that are "hidden" underneath.

Common physical symptoms of anger may include:

- Clenching your jaws or grinding your teeth

- Headache

- Stomachache

- Increased and rapid heart rate

- Sweating, especially your palms

- Feeling hot in the neck/face

- Shaking or trembling

- Dizziness

EXPLORING ANGER

· · · · · ·

Everyone experiences anger; it's a natural part of being human. This worksheet will help you to better understand your own anger and begin to find ways to manage those feelings when you have them.

List the things, circumstances, or thoughts that make you angry.

1. _____

2. _____

3. _____

4. _____

5. _____

6. _____

Now go back and rate them all, using #1 for the hardest situation and #6 for the easiest to manage. Pick a situation that you labeled as #1 or #2 (one of your hardest, most anger-provoking situations) and answer the following questions with that situation in mind:

What are some of the thoughts you have in this situation? (Thoughts might include things like: "I am going to be rejected or hurt, I am going to look foolish, or I am going to be treated unfairly.")

_____

_____

_____

What are some of the feelings (emotional and physical) you have in this situation? (Physical feelings might include: clenched teeth, flushed face, or stomachache. Emotional feelings might include: irritated, overwhelmed, or exasperated.)

_____

_____

_____

Now, consider *all* of the situations you previously listed that cause anger, as well as any others you can think of, and respond to the following questions:

How do you usually respond when you are feeling angry? What actions do you usually take?

_____

_____

_____

How do members of your family respond when they are angry? What about your friends? Take a moment and think about how you witness other people in your life acting when they are angry.

_____

_____

_____

UNDERSTANDING MY ANGER

• • • • • •

On the "Exploring Anger" worksheet, you identified several situations that make you angry. Use the following chart to look at those situations a little more closely. **For each situation, fill out the chart to identify the feelings (physical sensations and emotions), thoughts and worries, and actions that most often accompany that situation.** Then, imagine how you would like to handle the situation, and fill in the final column for what you wish would happen in that situation.

Situation	What I feel (Physical sensations and emotions)	What I think (Thoughts and worries)	What I do (Actions)	What I wish would happen
1.				
2.				
3.				

ANGER THERMOMETER

• • • • • •

Using a thermometer is one way to measure how intense a certain feeling is at any given time. Think about your anger when you use the following thermometer.

As you think about your anger, see if you can think of words that describe how the anger feels at 25, 50, 75, and 100% intensity. For example, 25% might be "Irritated," 50% might be "Upset," 75% might be "Really angry," and 100% could be "Enraged." For each of these intensities, please note how you notice the anger in your body. For example, when some people feel angry, they may feel their face flush, their muscles tense, their heart rate increase, and they may notice energy in their arms and legs.

Once you have filled in your thermometer, you can use it at any time to assess how you are feeling with regard to your anger.

Anger

— 100%   At 100% I feel: _____

My body cues are: _____

— 75%

At 75% I feel: _____

— 50%   My body cues are: _____

— 25%   At 50% I feel: _____

My body cues are: _____

At 25% I feel: _____

My body cues are: _____

TRACKING MY ANGER TRIGGERS

· · · · · ·

Over the course of the next week, pay attention to your feelings and what is happening right before or when you experience anger. At the end of each day, write down one anger trigger, and rate the intensity of your anger on a scale of 1–10 (with 1 being very little anger, and 10 being very intense anger).

Monday

Trigger: _____

Anger Rating: _____

Tuesday

Trigger: _____

Anger Rating: _____

Wednesday

Trigger: _____

Anger Rating: _____

Thursday

Trigger: _____

Anger Rating: _____

Friday

Trigger: _____

Anger Rating: _____

Saturday

Trigger: _____

Anger Rating: _____

Sunday

Trigger: _____

Anger Rating: _____

PRACTICING SELF-COMPASSION

• • • • • •

One of the ways that we can manage stress in our lives is through the practice of self-compassion. Often, we treat ourselves (through our actions or the things that we say to ourselves) in a way that is unkind. For example, when we make a mistake, we may think, "I'm such an idiot!" or something similar – when we would never say that to someone we love or care about deeply.

In contrast, when we practice **self-compassion**, we treat ourselves with the kindness we would show to a friend or a loved one, instead of using negative, judgmental thoughts and behaviors. **We recognize and accept that we are not perfect, and nobody else is either!**

• Think of a time that you made a mistake or did something that you felt was "wrong," which caused you to become upset with yourself. What happened? How did you react? What did you think and say to yourself?

_____

_____

_____

• If you told a friend or a loved one what happened, what would they say to you?

_____

_____

_____

• What would you say to a friend if they did the exact same thing you did?

_____

_____

_____

• Think of someone you really look up to and admire. What would they say to you?

_____

_____

_____

• Looking over all of your answers, how might you change how you think and act the next time something similar occurs in order to practice self-compassion?

_____

_____

_____

CHANGING SELF-TALK

· · · · · ·

The first step to changing how you talk to yourself is to begin noticing when you are being self-critical. Although this sounds easy, sometimes we are so used to being harsh or negative to ourselves that we don't even notice when it's happening. **Begin practicing changing this self-talk**.

1. Pay attention to the words you use when you are talking to yourself. These words are usually in your own mind, but sometimes we all find ourselves talking out loud to ourselves – and often this includes criticism! Notice any specific phrases you use. You might even be able to identify an internal "tone of voice" when you are engaging in negative self-talk. Write down examples of this.

_____

_____

_____

_____

2. Start to think about the feelings that are connected to your negative self-talk. Try acknowledging those feelings in a kind way. This might sound something like, "I know you are worried about doing poorly on the test, but this worry is causing you unnecessary pain," or "I understand that you are afraid about getting hurt, but this fear is causing you unnecessary pain." If you're having a hard time figuring out what to say, think about what you would say to a friend, and then finish the sentence by naming the feeling and adding "X is causing you unnecessary pain." It may also help to speak to yourself as "you" rather than as "I."

_____

_____

_____

_____

3. Think about how you can re-phrase the initial criticism you used by choosing a more positive perspective. Often, it helps to think about what you have learned from the situation, how you might handle the situation differently in the future, or what you might do to settle or resolve the situation in a more positive manner. Try using the language and "voice" of the compassionate friend you worked on in #2. It may also help to practice this while giving yourself a hug or a gentle squeeze.

_____

_____

_____

_____

POSITIVE SELF-TALK

· · · · · ·

How we talk to ourselves has a big impact on how we feel. Indeed, when our minds get stuck in negative thinking, we are actually increasing stress for ourselves. Given this, one way to help ourselves self-regulate is to use positive self-talk, especially in times of stress. As human beings, we all have strengths and challenges. Even if we don't see it right away, these inner strengths are present within us. These inner strengths are the skills, talents, and knowledge that we bring with this – and these can form the basis of positive self-talk.

Here are some ways that you can use positive self-talk to change your mood and your reactions when faced with a challenge:

- Say something positive to yourself every day, such as: "I am good at…", "I am working on…", or "It is okay."

- Picture yourself in a future situation that is positive, such as doing well on a test without worrying, or feeling comfortable making a new friend.

- Remember things that you have done well in the past, being as specific as possible. You might even want to keep a journal of "I did this!" to remind yourself of when you've been successful.

- Ask yourself how much your current challenge will matter in the future, thinking about one month from now, six months from now, one year from now, and five years from now.

- Make a recording of yourself saying supportive, positive things to yourself. If you don't feel ready to make this recording, ask someone you trust to do this for you.

- When facing a challenge, ask yourself if you are realistically in control of the things that are happening. If you can't control the situation (such as whether it rains tomorrow or not), then try practicing deep breathing for a few minutes and envision yourself letting the challenge or worry go.

PROBLEM SOLVING

· · · · · ·

One of the best ways to address stress (and decrease it!) is to develop skills in problem solving. When you have a plan that outlines what your goals are, it is easier to figure out the specific steps that you may need to take. This helps with self-regulation: Once you have identified a clear path to follow, you are better able to put it into practice. In turn, you are less likely to feel stressed (and when you are, you can use the tools we've already reviewed).

The following chart is intended to help you discover these details by identifying the "what, why, where, when, how, who" behind your goals.

WHAT	• What is my goal? What are the facts? • What resources do I need? • What goals have been suggested to me by someone else?
WHY	• Why do I want this? • Why do I need to solve this? • Why did this situation arise? • Why has this been suggested to me?
WHERE	• Where did this situation arise? • Where did this impact me? • Where does this impact others? • Does the "where" matter?
WHEN	• When did this situation arise? • When does it need to be addressed? • When do I need to take action? • When do I ask for help or support?
HOW	• How can I get more information? • How can the situation change? • How would someone else describe the problem?
WHO	• Who am I trying to please? • Who is involved? • Who can I talk with? • Who can give me an objective opinion?

TIME MANAGEMENT

· · · · · ·

Chances are, you have a busy life: school, friends, family, and maybe even a job that take up your time. However, it's also important to make time for relaxation and fun, as well as for healthy eating and getting enough sleep. Many people have a hard time balancing all of their obligations, and often the things that get left out are the very things that help us stay healthy and happy.

Learning to create a prioritized to-do list can really make a difference. It can help you stay organized and decrease the stress that comes from having too much to do and too little time. When you are able to determine a plan to finish what you need to get done, you are less likely to experience the sense of increased stress (and feeling of being overwhelmed) that results from feeling like you have too much to do. Managing and prioritizing your time in this manner is actually a preventive self-regulation strategy (similar to problem solving).

First, decide whether you want to create a daily prioritized list or a weekly one. Templates for both types of lists are provided on the following pages. One thing to think about is that although knowing what you have to do over the course of a month is helpful, it can usually be way too big of a list. When a list is too big, it can be overwhelming, which results in much less actually getting done.

- Whether you are doing a daily list or a weekly list, start by writing down all the tasks that you have to do. If one task is really big, try breaking it into smaller pieces. For example, instead of writing "Do all my homework," try breaking it down by subject.

- Re-look at your list and figure out if any tasks are due earlier than others. Then, estimate how much time each task will take to accomplish. Remember to be realistic when you do this part, and also consider whether or not you need any outside resources, such as help from someone else, supplies, etc.

- Next, review what tasks you need to do, and give each a priority rating, using #1 for the most important task, #2 for slightly less important, etc. It's okay to have two or three items with the same priority rating.

- Finally, re-do your list in priority order, starting with the highest priority items. Since you've already estimated how long each task will take, consider doing the shortest #1 priority task first. Doing so will increase your chances of success as you start checking tasks off your to-do list.

PRIORITIZED TASK LIST: DAILY

· · · · · ·

	HIGH PRIORITY TASKS
☐	Example: Study for test
☐	
☐	
☐	
☐	

	MEDIUM PRIORITY TASKS
☐	Example: Clean my room
☐	
☐	
☐	

	LOW PRIORITY TASKS
☐	Example: Go shopping
☐	
☐	

	ADDITIONAL TASKS
☐	
☐	
☐	

PRIORITIZED TASK LIST: WEEKLY

• • • • • •

HIGH PRIORITY TASKS	DUE DATE
☐ Example: Study for test	5/13
☐	
☐	
☐	
☐	

MEDIUM PRIORITY TASKS	DATE DUE
☐ Example: Clean my room	by Saturday
☐	
☐	
☐	

LOW PRIORITY TASKS	DATE DUE
☐ Example: Go shopping	Just for fun, so no date
☐	
☐	

ADDITIONAL TASKS	DUE DATE
☐	
☐	
☐	

INCREASE POSITIVE FEELINGS

Teenagers who have experienced trauma have many, and varied, emotional reactions to the traumatic experience itself, as well as to the world in general in the aftermath of the trauma. Teens who have experienced traumatic events frequently endorse feelings of anger, sadness, depression, and anxiety. They may lose interest in relationships and activities that they previously enjoyed, isolate themselves from family and friends, appear moody and irritable, or explode in response to minor stressors. Emotional numbness and dissociation are also not uncommon in individuals who have experienced abuse (SAMHSA, 2014). Teens may describe feeling disconnected from others and may experience a limited range of feelings (e.g., feeling only anger and sadness and unable to feel happiness or love). In more extreme cases, teens who have experienced trauma may exhibit symptoms of dissociation, such as "spacing out" for periods of time; feeling disconnected from their body, as if it is numb or belongs to someone else (depersonalization); or feeling as if their surroundings or events are unreal or unfamiliar (derealization).

Because of the many ways in which trauma impacts the emotions of teens, increasing an individual's experience of positive feelings is an important component of treatment for trauma (Spinazzola, 2010). Enhancing positive affect combats many negative outcomes of trauma by increasing the adolescent's "sense of self-worth, esteem, and positive self-appraisal through the cultivation of personal creativity, imagination, future orientation, achievement, competence, mastery-seeking, community-building and the capacity to experience pleasure" (Cook et al., 2005, p. 395).

Despite the common perception that happiness is outside of one's control, research from the field of positive psychology has demonstrated that individuals do have the ability to impact their overall feelings of happiness and well-being (Seligman, Steen, Park, & Nansook, 2005). In particular, research has found that certain interventions – such as performing new and different activities that cultivate your character strengths – produce long-term increases in happiness and decreases in depressive symptoms (Seligman et al., 2005). Even more heartening is the discovery that many of the behaviors that lead to increased happiness are simple, daily practices that can be done in very little time. **Engaging in gratitude practices, embracing creativity, savoring the positive**, and **cultivating your personal strengths** have all been found to make a difference in enhancing positive emotions (Seligman, 2002). The implications of this line of research, frequently referred to as positive psychology, is compelling in its own right.

The potential impact of positive psychology practices for adolescents is even more exciting. **Positive affect and subjective well-being in teenagers are correlated with improved learning, increased creative thinking, and decreased depression** (Seligman et al., 2009). Studies have demonstrated that adolescents can learn skills to increase happiness, and students who are taught positive psychology practices demonstrate improved academic performance, as well as decreased symptoms of depression and anxiety (Seligman et al., 2009; Waters, 2011). Some research even suggests that positive psychology interventions for adolescents who are at risk for (or are exhibiting) psychiatric symptoms can decrease maladaptive behaviors and increase life satisfaction (Lyons et al., 2014).

Gratitude practice involves intentionally noticing and feeling thankful for the positive things in your life, no matter how small. Research has demonstrated that one of the most effective ways to increase happiness is through the practice of gratitude. Specifically, grateful teens (compared to their less grateful peers) are happier and more satisfied with their lives, their friends, their family, and themselves. They report more hope, greater engagement with hobbies, higher grades at school, and less envy and depression (Froh et al., 2010). Additionally, gratitude practices have been tied to improved physical health outcomes, such as lower blood pressure, and increased social outcomes, such as improved quality of relationships.

Engaging in creative or artistic activities has also been found to result in lower stress levels, decreased symptoms of depression, and increased overall well-being for adolescents (Tamannaeifar & Motaghedifard, 2014). Making art may be particularly beneficial to individuals because not only is it enjoyable, but it can also facilitate the development of mindfulness. In particular, when the focus of creativity or artistic expression is on the *process* rather than the product, teens can build skills for staying in the present moment rather than focusing on the past or future. Creative expression also helps them practice non-judgmental observation and acceptance of their own mental process. In addition, art can provide a powerful modality through which individuals can express and process their emotions. Creative expression and art provide a non-verbal modality to process and express emotions, which teens may find difficult or reluctant to talk about directly. Creativity may even play a role in resilience to stressful situations. For example, one study demonstrated a link between creativity and overall well-being following individuals who survived the trauma of Hurricane Katrina (Metzel, 2009).

Research has found that another great way to boost long-term happiness involves **savoring the positive** (Seligman, 2002). **Savoring is the deliberate skill of drawing attention to positive experiences and sensations in order to prolong the good feeling.** Studies have demonstrated that teens can "maximize" a positive experience by sharing, marking, or celebrating the event, or reflecting on the event and the positive emotions with which it was associated. Indeed, adolescents who maximize positive events in this manner have been shown to exhibit more sustained positive feelings about that event, up to a full week later (Gentzler, Morey, Palmer, & Chit, 2013).

Last, research has found that **engaging in jobs, activities, and pursuits that utilize your personal strengths enhances feelings of purpose and life satisfaction** (Seligman, 2002). One reason for this is because individuals are more likely to value endeavors that align with and that regularly cultivate their core personal strengths. In fact, research indicates that one of the best ways to boost long-term happiness is to use your strengths in new ways and situations, rather than focusing on your weaknesses. Studies have demonstrated that interventions that focus on helping teens identify and utilize their character strengths can lead to improved school performance, decreased behavioral difficulties at school, enhanced social relationships, and increased academic motivation (Grunhauz & Castro Solano, 2014).

HOW TO INCORPORATE THE INCREASE POSITIVE FEELINGS WORKSHEETS

The worksheets in this section are designed to offer concrete strategies to increase positive affect. These activities are based on the large and growing body of research within positive psychology demonstrating that individuals, including adolescents, do have the ability to impact their overall feelings of happiness and that a shift in this area can lead to profound improvements in overall well-being, social and academic functioning, and even physical health.

The specific exercises included in this section are designed to facilitate the development of skills in the areas that have been found to increase positive feelings in most people: practicing gratitude, engaging creativity, savoring the positive, and understanding and utilizing personal strengths. For each of these skills, several options for practice are included. Teens should be encouraged to try the various exercises in each area to discover their own preferences – with the goal of developing new habits that will increase their experience of positive affect and overall well-being.

Many of these activities encourage the teen to develop and implement a short-term behavioral change and monitor how this change impacts their mood. It can be helpful to encourage the teenage client to view these activities as mini-experiments, wherein they approach the activity with a sense of curiosity. However, it is also important to remember that not every activity will work for every individual, and some of the strategies will work better at one point in time than another. Ideally, adolescents who complete these exercises will identify what works well for them, and after experiencing the positive benefits, be encouraged to make longer-term changes in their behavior.

When completing these activities, some teens may struggle to identify their own strengths, believing instead that they do not have any strengths. However, the exercises in this section provide a framework to assist the teen in exploring and discovering their strengths (because *everyone* has strengths). Similarly, some adolescents will express resistance to the creativity activities, perhaps due to concerns that they are not "good at art." In these cases, it can be beneficial to help the teen remember that the goal of the creative exercises is the process, not the product. Regardless of the outcome, they will benefit simply from engaging in the practice.

GRATITUDE

• • • • • •

What is Gratitude?

Gratitude is showing appreciation for something that is valuable to you.

Why Does Gratitude Matter?

People who practice gratitude have been shown to be happier and more satisfied with their lives, *even if nothing else in their life changes.* Practicing gratitude also leads to more hope, improved social relationships, improved grades, and decreased symptoms of depression.

What Does it Mean to "Practice" Gratitude?

Gratitude is a skill that we can learn, and it requires practice just like any other skill. You don't learn how to ride a bike without practice, and you won't learn gratitude without practice either! Practicing gratitude involves making an *active* choice about how you chose to see the world and your life.

How Can I Practice Gratitude?

• Keep a daily gratitude journal.

• Pay attention throughout the day to the things that you appreciate in your life.

• Stop to say a genuine "thank you" to people who do something nice for you or help you in any way, no matter how small.

• Give thanks before your meals. Think about all of the people who made your meal possible, from the people who grew the food to those who prepared it for you.

• Send a thank you message to someone who was kind to you today.

MY GRATITUDE JOURNAL

· · · · · ·

In order to begin practicing gratitude, keep a journal about something you are grateful for each day, and fill it out for the next week. If you are not sure what to write about, here are some ideas:

- What is something you are grateful to have learned today?
- What was the best part of your day?
- How did someone make your day better or make you smile?
- What song did you hear today that made you happy?
- Who is a person or pet you are grateful for?

Date: _____

Date: _____

Date: _____

Date: _____

Date: _____

Date: _____

Date: _____

SMALL ACTS OF GRATITUDE

• • • • • •

1. Keep a daily gratitude journal.

2. Take time to tell someone you love them and why.

3. Take a walk outside and notice the beauty in the nature around you.

4. Do something nice for a friend you are grateful for.

5. Watch inspiring videos that remind you of the good in the world.

6. Do a random act of kindness.

7. Steer clear of gossip.

8. Compliment someone.

9. Try to avoid complaining for a whole hour (or day).

10. Avoid violent media.

11. Create a collage with pictures of people and things you are grateful for.

12. Be thankful when you learn something new.

13. See the opportunity to learn from difficult situations.

14. Take a timeout once per day to practice gratitude.

15. Focus on your strengths.

16. Make gratitude a part of each meal: Say a prayer or a word of thanks before eating.

17. Share your thoughts on gratitude on social media.

18. Teach a friend or family member about the benefits of gratitude.

19. Notice and appreciate the little things you do every day to take care of yourself.

20. Ask yourself what you can learn from your failures.

DAILY GRATITUDE PRACTICE

· · · · · ·

Each day for the next week, select one gratitude practice to use throughout the day. Use the following record to keep track of your daily gratitude practice.

Day 1 Date: _____

Gratitude practice of the day:

_____

Day 2 Date: _____

Gratitude practice of the day:

_____

Day 3 Date: _____

Gratitude practice of the day:

_____

Day 4 Date: _____

Gratitude practice of the day:

_____

Day 5 Date: _____

Gratitude practice of the day:

_____

Day 6 Date: _____

Gratitude practice of the day:

_____

Day 7 Date: _____

Gratitude practice of the day:

_____

DAILY GRATITUDE PRACTICE REFLECTION

• • • • • •

At the end of your week, answer these questions by circling the number that best corresponds with your response:

1. I practiced my daily gratitude:

    1 – Never

    2 – Rarely

    3 – Sometimes

    4 – Often

    5 – Always

2. Practicing gratitude was:

    1 – Very difficult

    2 – Difficult

    3 – Neutral

    4 – Easy

    5 – Very easy

3. After practicing gratitude for one week, I feel:

    1 – Much worse

    2 – Somewhat worse

    3 – About the same

    4 – Somewhat better

    5 – Much better

Total score = _____

*Note your total score for these three questions. If it is not as high as you would like it to be, try this activity again and see if your score increases.

GRATITUDE LETTER

. . . . . .

Think of someone who you are grateful for in your life. It may be a family member, friend, teacher, or other important person in your life.

Using the template on the following page, write a letter to that person explaining why you are grateful for him or her. Be as specific as you can!

After you have written the letter, it is your choice whether or not you'd like to share the letter with that person. Keep in mind that most people like to feel like they have been helpful to others, so receiving your gratitude letter may really make that person's day!

An even bigger challenge would be to actually read your letter of gratitude to the other person, face to face. Just imagine how that person would feel hearing in your own words and voice what a difference he or she has made in your life. Not only that, but you will have the benefit of knowing that what you did (in sharing your letter) was helpful too. That's a win-win!

. . .

Here are a few prompts to get you started with your gratitude letter:

What does/did the person do that helped you in some way?

How do/did you feel when this individual helps/helped you?

What is special about this person that you value?

What do you enjoy doing together?

How do you feel when you are around this person?

. . .

Date _____

Dear _____

_____

_____

_____

_____

_____

_____

_____

_____

_____

_____

_____

_____

_____

Sincerely,

_____

CREATIVITY: DID YOU KNOW?

· · · · · ·

Creativity is a set of skills that **can be learned.**

Creativity helps with **self-expression.**

Practicing creativity **improves your problem-solving skills.**

Practicing creativity can **increase your confidence.**

People who engage in creative activities have been shown to have a **longer lifespan** than those who do not.

Creativity **decreases stress, increases joy,** and **improves quality of life.**

Creativity **improves your ability to focus.**

SOME THOUGHTS ON CREATIVITY

• • • • • •

You can't use up creativity. The more you use, the more you have.

– Maya Angelou

Once we believe in ourselves, we can risk curiosity, wonder, spontaneous delight or any experience that reveals the human spirit.

– E. E. Cummings

We don't make mistakes, just happy little accidents.

– Bob Ross

The thing about creativity is, people are going to laugh at it. Get over it.

– Twyla Tharp

Originality is the best form of rebellion.

– Mike Sasso

The worst enemy to creativity is self-doubt.

– Sylvia Plath

Art is not a handicraft, it is the transmission of feeling the artist has experienced.

– Leo Tolstoy

Whether you succeed or not is irrelevant, there is no such thing. Making your unknown known is the important thing.

– Georgia O'Keeffe

Don't think about making art, just get it done. Let everyone else decide if it's good or bad, whether they love it or hate it. While they are deciding, make even more art.

– Andy Warhol

Creativity takes courage.

– Henri Matisse

To be an artist is to believe in life.

– Henry Moore

The world always seems brighter when you've just made something that wasn't there before.

– Neil Gaiman

Every child is an artist. The problem is how to remain an artist once we grow up.

– Pablo Picasso

REMEMBERING YOUR CREATIVITY

• • • • • •

You are a creative being! Just by virtue of the fact that you are human, you are creative. Use the space provided to write yourself a message that will help you remember your creativity. You can select a favorite quote about creativity from the previous pages, or write your own message to yourself—whatever will help you remember that you are a creative being.

Then, decorate the page however you like. When you are done, hang or save this paper somewhere where you can easily see it as a reminder whenever you doubt your own creativity!

WAYS TO BE CREATIVE

· · · · · ·

Be curious

Make your own flower arrangement

Write song lyrics or a rap

Paint

Create a new recipe and cook or bake it

Plant some flowers

Write a short story

Draw

Color

Think outside of the box

Create or color a mandala

Journal

Sculpt something out of clay

Doodle

Sign up for a class to learn a new skill

Dance

Daydream

Sing

Play with playdough

Try out for a play

Learn to play an instrument

Write a poem

Ask questions

EXPLORING MY CREATIVITY

· · · · · · ·

When I was little, my favorite type of art was:

_____

_____

_____

I used to love to play:

_____

_____

_____

One time when I found a creative solution to a problem was:

_____

_____

_____

Something I created myself was:

_____

_____

_____

I have always been curious about:

_____

_____

_____

EPHEMERAL NATURE ART

· · · · · ·

Ephemeral: Lasting for a very short time

One of the challenges of creating art is that we often get overly focused on creating a "final product" that looks a certain way. While there is nothing wrong with this as a goal for your artwork, we run the risk of becoming upset or feeling like we have failed if the final product does not look exactly how we expected or wanted it to.

It is important to remember that being creative simply for creativity's sake is enough. The process of creating art and being creative is the goal. One way to practice expressing your creativity without worrying about the end product is to create ephemeral art. **Ephemeral art is art that is not meant to last. It is meant to be created, observed, and then to gradually fade away.**

Here is a simple way to create your own ephemeral nature art:

- Go for a walk outside and collect bits and pieces that you think are beautiful, interesting, or otherwise catch your attention. Bring along a small basket or bag to carry what you find. Things to look for include, but are not limited to: rocks and stones, sticks, leaves, flowers, flower petals, and feathers.

- Once you have collected at least 20 to 30 items, find a spot where you would like to work. You can choose a place where others are likely to see your work, or a place where your work will remain private, to be seen only by you.

- Take all of your items out of the bag or basket and begin to arrange them on the ground in any way that you like.

- If you are not sure how to start, try using your objects to create a circle. Circles are a form that are frequently found in nature and are sometimes used by artists to signify the cyclical nature of life or the interconnectedness of the world.

- You can add or take away items as you create your artwork.

- Once you feel that your art is complete, take a moment to observe your art.

- Leave your art outdoors – knowing that, soon, the items will be scattered by the wind, rain, or creatures that come along. Your art will not last, but you were nonetheless successful in being creative. Congratulations!

Some other ideas for ephemeral art for you to try:

- Build a sand castle or draw something in the sand.
- Build a snowman or use colored water to paint on the snow.
- Artfully arrange the food on your plate or serving dish.
- Draw on the sidewalk or pavement with chalk.

ONE INCH ART

• • • • • •

Making art can be intimidating, especially if you don't consider yourself creative or artistic. And even if you are an artist, sometimes you simply don't have the time to create a masterpiece.

One Inch Art – or "inchies" as it is sometimes called – is a creative solution to this problem. The idea is to create a very small piece of art that can be done quickly and easily. These are also a great type of "portable" art that you can do on-the-go.

The only rule for One Inch Art is that you create your artwork within a one-inch square. You may use whatever art medium appeals to you or whatever you have on hand, such as crayons, markers, pens, pencils, stickers, paint, or any other medium that comes to mind.

If you don't know where to start, try:

• Drawing a little doodle and adding some color
• Creating a pattern within the box
• Writing a word in the box and then decorating it
• Filling the box only with colors without worrying about making "something"

Here are a few one-inch squares for you to practice making One Inch Art. You can always create your own on whatever type of paper you prefer.

SAVORING THE POSITIVE

Savoring the positive is the skill and practice of drawing your attention to the positive experiences in your life as a way to improve your mood. **Ways to savor the positive include:**

- Sharing the experience with a loved one
- Reflecting on the experience and its associated positive feelings
- Journaling about the experience and feelings
- Marking or celebrating the experience

It is important to remember that savoring the positive applies to good experiences, big and small. Birthdays, holidays, graduations, and milestones are all big, positive experiences that can be savored. However, small, positive experiences, which occur much more frequently, can also be savored, such as the taste of a favorite food, sharing a laugh with a friend, or the feeling of sunshine on your face on a warm summer day.

Studies have shown that when you savor the positive, you can extend the good feelings up to an entire week!

EVERYDAY PLEASURES

· · · · · ·

"We are all so busy chasing the extraordinary that we forget to stop and be grateful for the ordinary."

– Brené Brown

The purpose of this activity is to help you remember to savor the small things that make you happy and bring you joy each day. Here is a list of just a few simple everyday pleasures. Add some of your own to the list!

Warm fuzzy blanket	Hug from a loved one
Laughing with a friend	Listening to your favorite song
A familiar smell	Beautiful sunrise or sunset
The feeling of sunshine on your skin	Receiving an unexpected compliment
Making someone smile	The taste of cold ice cream on a hot day
The feel of grass or sand on your bare feet	Spending time with people you cherish
Listening to the rain	Finishing something on your to-do list
Flowers	Your favorite movie
Seeing a rainbow	Cuddling with your pet
Balloons	Reading a favorite book from your childhood
A good hair day	New school supplies
Sitting by the fireplace	Talking to a good friend

PLANNING FOR THE POSITIVE

• • • • • •

We can't always control what happens in our lives, but we can make choices that increase the likelihood that we will experience something positive in each day. One way to do this is to *intentionally* schedule positive things that you can do in 10 minutes or less that will bring you a little sense of happiness or pleasure.

In order to add something positive to your schedule, use the monthly calendar on the next page and fill it out as follows:

• First, fill in the month and its corresponding dates.

• Next, write in any important events that you know will be happening in the coming month – whether they are positive, neutral, or negative. Examples of these events could include birthdays, scheduled activities or sports, assignment due dates, or any social plans you might have.

• Finally, go through the calendar and add three to four simple pleasures each week. These should be activities that, while easy to do, bring you happiness or pleasure.

PLANNING FOR THE POSITIVE MONTH: _____

. . . .

SUNDAY	MONDAY	TUESDAY	WEDNESDAY	THURSDAY	FRIDAY	SATURDAY

WHAT BRINGS ME JOY: THEN & NOW

• • • • • •

For this activity, you are going to take a trip down memory lane. Take a few moments to think about all of the things that you enjoyed when you were younger *that still bring you joy* today. It could be favorite books, songs, or TV characters. It might include a favorite blanket or special stuffed animal. Hobbies that you enjoyed as a child and still like now could also go on your list.

Use the following space to summarize all the things that bring you joy, then and now. You may choose to write a list, draw, or even create a collage with photographs or magazine images.

UNCOVERING YOUR STRENGTHS

· · · · · ·

Strengths are those traits that make you unique, such as your talents, knowledge, and skills. These are the aspects of your character or personality that help you to be successful in various types of situations.

However, people sometimes have difficulty recognizing their own strengths. You might even think that you do not have *any* strengths. However, this is not true! Everyone has strengths, and those strengths vary from person to person. While you may be good at math and science, another friend may be a talented musician or artist. **No strength is better or worse than another.** It is the diversity of strengths between individuals when brought together that contributes to a fully functioning and interesting community.

The following questions will help you to uncover your strengths.

1. What is something that you do very easily that others may not always find to be easy?

_____

_____

_____

2. What do others often ask you for your help with?

_____

_____

_____

3. Think about the things that you love to do most. What is it about these activities that you enjoy? What strengths might these interests suggest?

_____

_____

_____

4. Think of a time when you successfully faced a challenge. What helped you to overcome this challenge?

_____

_____

_____

5. What are you best at in school? What makes you successful in this area?

_____

_____

_____

6. What do your friends and family say that they admire about you? If you are not sure, ask them what they see as your strengths. You may be surprised by some of their answers!

_____

_____

_____

IDENTIFYING YOUR STRENGTHS

· · · · · ·

Now that you have spent some time uncovering your strengths, **look at the following list of strengths and circle all of those that apply to you.** Are there any you would add to this list?

Adventurous	Flexible	Lively	Problem solving
Ambitious	Focused	Logical	Respect
Artistic	Friendliness	Love	Responsibility
Athletic	Generosity	Love of learning	Self-assurance
Charm	Gratitude	Modesty	Self-control
Communicative	Helpfulness	Motivation	Seriousness
Compassionate	Honesty	Observant	Social skills
Common sense	Hope	Open minded	Spirituality
Confident	Humility	Optimistic	Spontaneous
Courage	Humor	Orderly	Straightforward
Creativity	Independence	Organization	Tactful
Critical thinking	Industriousness	Originality	Team oriented
Curiosity	Ingenuity	Outgoing	Thoughtful
Determination	Inspirational	Patient	Thrifty
Energetic	Integrity	Perseverance	Tolerant
Entertaining	Intelligence	Persistence	Trustworthy
Enthusiastic	Kindness	Persuasiveness	Warmth
Fair	Knowledgeable	Practical	Willpower
Fast	Leadership	Precise	Wisdom

PERSONAL STRENGTHS STORIES

· · · · · ·

In the previous activity, you learned to identify different types of strengths and explored your own personal strengths. For this activity, select three of your top strengths or three strengths that you most value. **For each of these strengths, think of a time when you demonstrated this characteristic, and then answer the following questions**:

1. Strength: _____

What was the situation? How specifically did you demonstrate this strength?

_____

_____

_____

_____

2. Strength: _____

What was the situation? How specifically did you demonstrate this strength?

_____

_____

_____

_____

3. Strength: _____

What was the situation? How specifically did you demonstrate this strength?

_____

_____

_____

_____

APPLYING YOUR STRENGTHS

• • • • • •

People who understand and apply their own strengths are more likely to be successful and more likely to achieve their own goals. These people tend to feel happier and have better self-esteem as well! **This activity will help you to think about how you can take advantage of your unique strengths and put them to work in your life**.

My top five personal strengths:

1. _____

2. _____

3. _____

4. _____

5. _____

Describe a time when you used your strengths to improve your relationships with others:

_____

_____

_____

Describe a time when you used your strengths to work toward a personal goal:

_____

_____

_____

Describe a time when you used your strengths to make a difference or give back to others:

_____

_____

_____

USING YOUR STRENGTHS TO MEET YOUR GOALS

• • • • • •

What is one current goal you have for yourself or your life?

_____

Identify at least three personal strengths and how you could use them to help you reach this goal:

1. **Strength:**

_____

How this strength can help me reach my goal:

_____

_____

_____

2. **Strength:**

_____

How this strength can help me reach my goal:

_____

_____

_____

3. **Strength:**

_____

How this strength can help me reach my goal:

_____

_____

_____

4. **Strength:**

_____

How this strength can help me reach my goal:

_____

_____

_____

NAME POEM

· · · · · ·

For this activity, you will be creating a poem using the letters of your first name. **For each letter in your name, think of one positive trait or characteristic about yourself that starts with that letter**. You can use your given name or a favorite nickname if you prefer. Here are two different examples:

A	Athletic
L	Loving
E	Energetic
X	eXtraordinary

B	Being fashionable
L	Love music
A	A good friend
K	Keeping organized
E	Every day I try my best

You can see how Alex was creative with the last letter since it was hard to find an appropriate word that starts with X. Blake used phrases instead of single words.

You can feel free to use phrases or words, whatever works best for you. Be creative, and use a thesaurus if you are having trouble thinking of a word for a specific letter in your name. When you are done, you may want to decorate the paper or add some drawings or stickers that reflect some of the unique aspects of yourself that make you YOU!

My Name

_____ _____

_____ _____

_____ _____

_____ _____

_____ _____

_____ _____

_____ _____

_____ _____

_____ _____

_____ _____

6

BUILDING HEALTHY RELATIONSHIPS

Dating violence – which is also frequently known as intimate partner violence, sexual violence, and gender-based violence – is defined as any physical, sexual, psychological, or emotional aggression that occurs within the context of a romantic relationship (Breiding, Basile, Smith, Black, & Mahendra, 2015). Unfortunately, dating violence continues to be on the rise with adolescents. For example, according to the 2015 National Youth Behavior Risky Survey, 16% of high school girls in the U.S. reported sexual dating violence in the past 12 months, and almost 12% of high school girls reported experiencing physical violence from a dating partner (Kann et al., 2016). This type of violence isn't limited to females, as 5% of male teens reported sexual violence and 7% reported physical violence within a dating relationship (Kann et al., 2016). Moreover, the CDC estimates that by age 18, 23% of females and 14% of males will have experienced dating violence (Breiding et al., 2014).

One factor that is associated with the rise of adolescent dating violence appears to be teen attitudes around dating violence. While it is true that adolescents tend to disapprove of dating violence in general, they may tend to have gender-based double standards. Specifically, research has found that teens who hold traditional gender norm beliefs are more likely to engage in interpersonal dating violence (Reyes, Foshee, Niolon, Reidy, & Hall, 2016). Similarly, other research suggests that adolescents may be more likely to rationalize dating violence perpetrated by females against their male partners. For example, some teens have suggested that females should not be punished for hitting males due to the belief that the male must have "deserved" it (Gallopin & Leigh, 2009).

For those adolescents who experience dating violence, the consequences can be high, including substance abuse, physical injury, depression, and difficulties in managing adult intimate relationships (Halpern, Oslak, Young, Martin, & Kupper, 2001). In addition, dating violence often disrupts a teen's ability to form healthy relationships. In the developmental period of adolescence, the relationships that teens have with those around them – including their romantic partners, parents, teachers, peers, and friends – provide the context for the development and refinement of healthy relationships. **Therefore, traumatic experiences (such as dating violence) can disrupt teenagers' ability to feel secure and engage in these critical relationships. In turn, they may be less able to tolerate feeling cared for, helped, and supported by others (Courtois & Ford, 2009).**

At the same time, though, teens' recovery in the aftermath of a traumatic experience is significantly dependent on the amount of trauma-related social support they receive (Cohen, Mannarino, & Deblinger, 2006). Therefore, adolescents who have experienced trauma, including that which occurs within the context of a romantic relationship, can benefit from developing skills to help them build a strong social support system and better manage interpersonal relationships. Through improved communication skills, including assertiveness, and healthy boundary setting, adolescents can decrease their vulnerability to future victimization and traumatization.

Importantly, this workbook is not geared to address the full range of prevention strategies regarding dating violence in adolescents. **Rather, the exercises in this workbook are meant as the initial step in defining and promoting healthy relationships for teens.** For further information on teen dating violence prevention and education, the CDC has developed a free training for those involved in working with adolescents, which can be found at https://vetoviolence.cdc.gov/apps/datingmatters/.

HOW TO INCORPORATE THE BUILDING HEALTHY RELATIONSHIP WORKSHEETS

The activities in this section focus on building the skills needed to form healthy relationships within the framework of a trauma-informed approach to treatment. As in the rest of the workbook, these exercises can be utilized in conjunction with all of the topics covered in other chapters.

The worksheets in this section cover assertive communication (including how to deal with criticism), understanding and setting boundaries, and identifying a healthy support system. The activities in this section may be introduced at any time in treatment and may need to be reviewed at various points during treatment as other skills are being developed and other symptoms are being addressed. Because healthy relationships form the context for normal adolescent development, building skills in this domain can facilitate adolescents' skill development in other areas as well.

It is our contention that understanding how to speak in an empowered manner and learning how to effectively respond across a variety of difficult situations (e.g., bullying, verbal aggression, criticism) forms the foundation of effective communication skills regardless of a history of trauma. Learning to understand, think about, and set clear boundaries is also a necessary skill that crosses all areas of this workbook.

MY SUPPORT SYSTEM

· · · · · ·

Social supports are the people in your life who support you, whether that be physically, emotionally, or in other ways. Different people may provide different types of support. A healthy social support system is an important resource to help you manage stress.

Use the diagram on the next page to identify people who provide you with the following types of support:

- **Material:** People who give you material support provide you with tangible things (such as food and clothing) and help you out when you need it (such as giving you a ride to your friend's house or cooking you a meal).

- **Emotional:** These people support you by demonstrating empathy, love, trust, and caring (such as a friend you can call when you are upset, or a mentor who empathizes when you are facing a difficult situation).

- **Informational:** People who provide informational support give you advice, suggestions, and information (such as a teacher who teaches you about the college admissions process, or a parent who offers you advice when you are facing a difficult decision).

You may also have people in your life who support you in multiple ways. Use the overlapping parts of the circles to identify those people who provide you with more than one type of support.

MAPPING MY SUPPORT SYSTEM

· · · · · ·

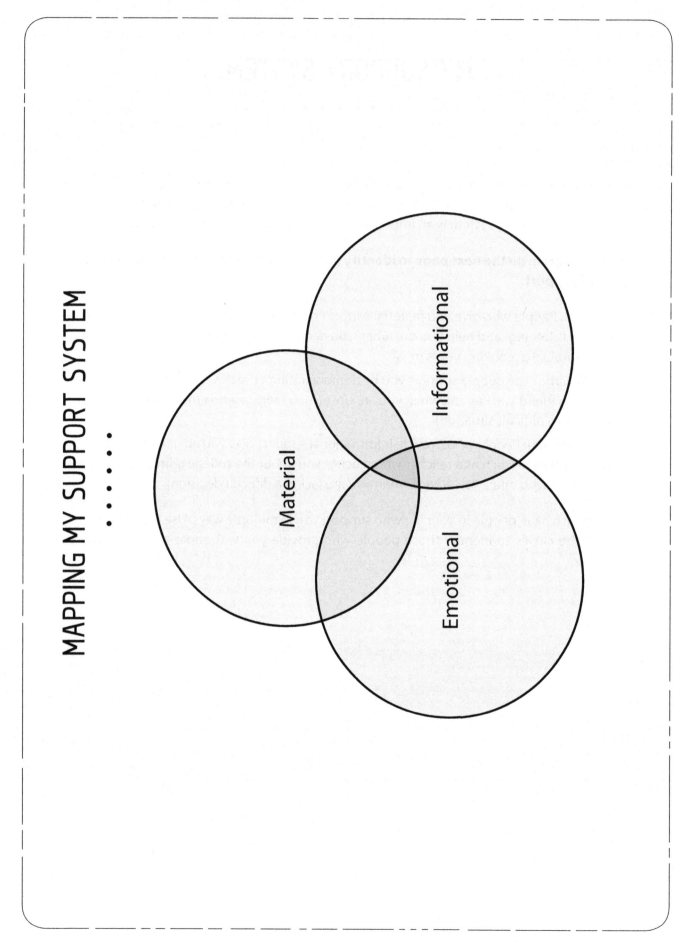

Material

Informational

Emotional

EVALUATING MY SUPPORT SYSTEM

. . . . . .

After you have completed the "Mapping My Support System" exercise, respond to the following questions to take a closer look at how your support system measures up.

Which type of support person was easiest to identify? Which was hardest? Why do you think this might be?

_____

_____

_____

When is it easiest to rely on your support system?

_____

_____

_____

When is it most difficult to rely on your support system?

_____

_____

_____

How do you feel about receiving support from others?

_____

_____

_____

Do you feel you have enough support people in each category? Are there any support people who are missing from your life right now?

_____

_____

_____

How might you go about increasing your social support system?

_____

_____

_____

What are some ways that you can let others know when you need support?

_____

_____

_____

ASSERTIVE COMMUNICATION

· · · · · ·

Being assertive involves being clear and confident about who you are and what you are doing. It does not involve aggressive, threatening, challenging, or highly defensive behaviors. When we communicate assertively, we do so both in terms of the words that we use, as well as the messages that we send with our bodies.

Assertive Body Communication Involves:

- Standing straight and tall (or sitting upright in your chair)
- Looking people in the eye when speaking with them
- Sitting in a relaxed, but businesslike manner
- Initiating conversation
- Speaking clearly in response to questions or in order to add information
- Remaining courteous and pleasant during the discussion

Body Communication That is NOT Assertive Involves:

- Not showing confidence
- Slumping when standing or sitting
- Not making eye contact with the person who is talking to you
- Trying to be inconspicuous (not noticed)
- Not taking initiative when speaking or responding to others
- Being rude or argumentative when communicating with others

Benefits of Assertive Communication:

- Others are more likely to respect you and your boundaries
- You are more likely to get your needs met
- You may feel more self-respect
- You can more easily respect others and their boundaries

HOW DO YOU COMMUNICATE
WITH YOUR BODY?

• • • • • •

Think about how you tend to hold your body or act when you feel uncomfortable, anxious, insecure, or threatened. List 3-5 ways that your body reflects your emotions:

1. _____

2. _____

3. _____

4. _____

5. _____

Think about how you tend to hold your body or act when you feel comfortable, relaxed, confident, or secure. List 3-5 ways your body reflects your emotions:

1. _____

2. _____

3. _____

4. _____

5. _____

Passive

Assertive

Aggressive

DEALING WITH CRITICISM

· · · · · ·

It's hard when someone criticizes us. No one wants to hear criticism – it usually doesn't feel good, and we often feel uncomfortable, bad, or less confident. However, using assertive communication to deal with criticism can really make a difference. **The following are three assertive choices you can make in order to handle a situation when you are on the receiving end of criticism:**

1. **Acknowledge any part of the criticism that is true.**
   - Sometimes we hear commentary from the other that is partly true, but the person has said "always" or "never." For example, the other person may say, "You never do your homework."
   - When this happens, it helps to acknowledge that *at times* you have engaged in the behavior. For example, you can reply by saying, "It's true that there are times when I haven't done my homework or when I've done it really quickly, without a lot of effort."
   - By owning up to the times or situations in which the person's criticism is true, you are better able to be assertive about what is going on *right now*.

2. **Own up to your mistakes.**
   - When you do something wrong – even if it's by mistake – you can use assertive communication to admit that you made a mistake.
   - Make sure that you use "I" statements and do not respond with "you" statements. For example, if you said something that hurt a friend's feelings, you could say, "I am sorry that what I said hurt you. I will try not to do it again."

3. **Ask for feedback.**
   - Ask what it is about your behavior that is bothering the person and do so in a courteous and polite manner.
   - If somebody continues to criticize you when it is not necessary, then ask what it is exactly that you are doing that is problematic.
   - When you ask for clarity while staying calm and polite, this allows you to better understand the other person's point-of-view.
   - For example, if your parent is upset by something you said but you are unsure why, you could ask, "I am sorry that I upset you. Can you please explain what was upsetting about it so I can avoid upsetting you next time?"

   No matter what, it's important to remember that criticism is about a behavior. It's NOT about your worth as a person.

ACCEPTING CRITICISM PRACTICE

· · · · · ·

Try using this worksheet to practice your ability to accept criticism by applying this skill to a real example from your life.

First, think of a time when someone gave you criticism. What criticism did they give you?

_____

_____

_____

How did you respond in this situation?

_____

_____

_____

Now, regardless of how you handled the situation when it happened, use the following chart to identify how you *could* have responded in this situation by making assertive choices.

Skill	Appropriate behavior	What I could have done/said
1. **Acknowledge any part of the criticism that is true.**	• Stay calm. Don't get angry and upset. • Say that I will make the changes.	

2. Own up to your mistakes.	• Don't blame someone else. • Say that I made a mistake. • Admit that there is a problem.	
3. Ask for feedback.	• Ask how I can correct it or say how I will correct it. • Ask what specific things I can do to improve. • Listen to advice from others. • Say what I will do. • Thank people who give me advice.	

Finally, reflect on how things might have been different in this situation if you had accepted the criticism and responded with assertive communication choices. Would you have felt any different? Might the situation have ended differently?

_____

_____

_____

SETTING BOUNDARIES

· · · · · ·

Personal boundaries are the limits, guidelines, or rules that we use to navigate our relationships with others. Boundaries are invisible barriers between you and other people. You can think about boundaries as the "fences" that control how close other people can get to you and how much of yourself you give to others. The following are different types of boundaries:

· **Physical boundaries** refer to the extent to which we permit physical closeness, touch, and personal space. For example, who is allowed to give you a hug?

· **Mental boundaries** apply to our thoughts, feelings, and values, and how we allow others to influence us. For example, whose advice do you value?

· **Emotional boundaries** are the way in which we distinguish our own emotions from those of someone else. Emotional boundaries also help us determine how much personal information we wish to share in any given situation. For example, if someone else is upset, do you allow their bad mood to influence your mood?

Here are a few important things to remember about boundaries:

· Boundaries are **individual**: Your boundaries will not be the same as someone else's.

· Boundaries may **vary** depending on the situation and the other people involved: You may be comfortable with a hug from a close family member but not from an acquaintance.

· Boundaries are **learned**: You may have learned certain boundaries based on your parents or family norms.

· Boundaries can be **changed**: You are in control of your own boundaries and can change them at any time.

Here are some questions to get you thinking about your personal boundaries.

What are some messages you have seen in the media about boundaries? For example, how do you see men respecting or not respecting women's boundaries in the media?

_____

_____

_____

What makes setting boundaries difficult or challenging? Are there certain situations where it is easier or harder to set boundaries?

_____

_____

_____

What are three of your own personal boundaries? Who do these boundaries apply to?

1. _____

2. _____

3. _____

Describe a time when you set a personal boundary. What was the situation? Who else was involved? How did you set the boundary? How did you feel after setting the boundary?

_____

_____

_____

CONTINUUM OF BOUNDARIES
· · · · · ·

Boundaries occur on a continuum, from very open to very rigid. Here is an example:

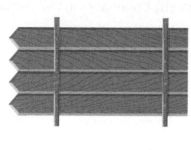

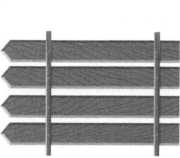

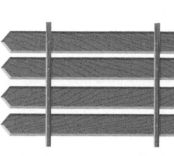

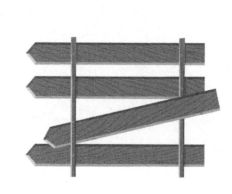

Very Rigid Boundaries
- Avoid sharing any personal details
- Unlikely to ask for help
- Disregard others' opinions
- Keep others at an emotional distance

Moderate Boundaries
- Able to share personal information in an appropriate way
- Able to offer help but also able to say "no" when necessary
- Don't compromise values for others
- Able to distinguish between own feelings and others' feelings, but still feel empathy

Very Open Boundaries
- Share lots of personal information
- Difficulty saying "no"
- Very influenced by other' opinions
- Tend to "take on" other's feelings

MY PERSONAL BOUNDARIES

· · · · · ·

The diagram below gives you a way to visualize your boundaries with different people. You are in the smallest circle in the middle. Put your name in this circle.

In the next circle, list the people with whom you have the most open boundaries.

These are the people you are **most comfortable** being close to – physically, emotionally, and mentally.

Use the next circle to list people you are **somewhat comfortable** being close to.

Finally, in the outer circle, list those people you are **least comfortable** being close to. These are the people with whom you have the most rigid boundaries.

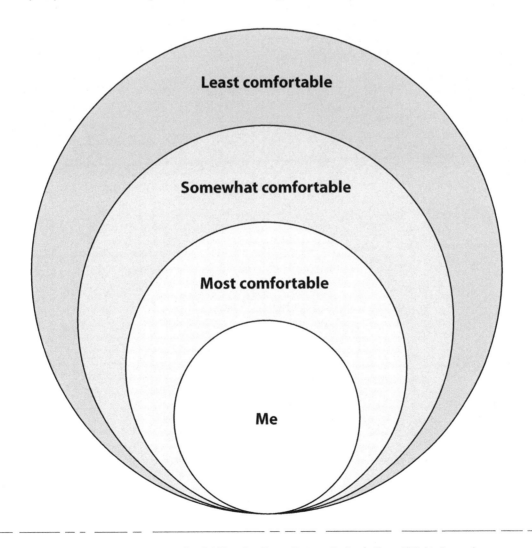

MAKING MEANING AFTER TRAUMA

One of the insidious ways that trauma impacts individuals is by altering their sense of meaning. Adolescents who have experienced trauma may subsequently tend to view the world in a pessimistic way, feel that their lives do not make sense or have purpose, feel despair or hopelessness, or feel doubtful about their ability to make positive changes (Spinazzola, 2010). These alterations can lead to longer-term symptoms, including depression and anxiety, which may persist even after the more acute symptoms related to the traumatic exposure have resolved.

The concept of "post-traumatic growth" is one way to conceptualize the protective aspects of making meaning after the experience of trauma. **Post-traumatic growth is essentially the positive change experienced as the result of a trauma or loss. In post-traumatic growth, individuals develop new understandings of themselves, their relationships, and the world.** They may have a new view of their personal strengths and see new possibilities for their own future (Tedeschi & Calhoun, 1996). Evidence of post-traumatic growth has been documented in survivors of combat, the Holocaust, divorce, bereavement, terroristic events, and major illness (Knapp & Robinson, 2017).

In children and adolescents specifically, positive expectations about their own competencies and positive expectations for their own future are associated with increased post-traumatic growth (Cryder, Kilmer, Tedeschi, & Calhoun, 2006). When a teen is able to see themselves as a competent person and can identify their strengths and ability to learn and implement skills, they have a much higher likelihood of overcoming the challenging effects of trauma. The specific tasks related to meaning making for adolescents include not only internal reflection and meaning making, but also external reflection and goal-directed behavior (Spinazzola, 2010). **Reflection is about connecting current experiences to prior learning (called scaffolding).** Reflection includes bringing information from all our sensory sources (visual, auditory, kinesthetic, and tactile). Reflecting means taking what you've learned and applying it to new situations. *Internal reflection* is self-knowledge – that is, paying attention to both *what* and *how* we are thinking. *External reflection* is taking in and applying others' comments, suggestions, and feedback. Ultimately, the goal of meaning making after trauma is to develop an identity that is not defined in terms of past traumas, but one that is centered around engagement in a meaningful life (Knapp & Robinson, 2017).

HOW TO INCORPORATE THE MAKING MEANING WORKSHEETS

The worksheets in this section provide structure to assist the teen in making meaning in their own life after the experience of trauma. This section includes activities to increase self-esteem through increased awareness of identity and values. Exercises are also included to assist adolescents in envisioning their own future, setting meaningful personal goals, and providing concrete structure for helping them achieve these goals.

The activities in this section may be especially helpful in the later phases of treatment, after the more impairing symptoms related to the trauma are becoming better managed. At this point in treatment, the focus may shift from helping adolescents manage their symptoms to beginning to construct a personal narrative that includes not only their struggles associated with the past trauma, but also a positive future supported by their own strengths and resilience. Rather than forcing the concept of post-traumatic growth in the early phases of treatment, the therapist may opt to wait until the adolescent has begun to recognize and acknowledge their own resilience. At that point, the teen may be more open to exploring ways to facilitate their own post-traumatic growth through the activities in this section.

In guiding adolescents through these activities, it can be helpful to remember that post-traumatic growth does not negate the stressful and difficult experiences of trauma. Rather, it is an approach that can help the teen to see "some good" as coming from their very difficult life experiences (Tedeschi & Calhoun, 1996). In this way, the teen can be both validated in their emotional response to the trauma and also encouraged to continue their growth in a positive direction.

SELF-ESTEEM SENTENCES

• • • • • •

Self-esteem is a reflection of how we think about ourselves. We are all human, and we each have strengths and areas for growth. Even when it seems like we don't have anything we're good at, we each have our own unique talents and abilities. **Complete the following sentences to learn more about yourself and reflect on your own strengths**. (Remember, we talked about identifying your personal strengths in Chapter 5, so feel free to review or look back at that section of the workbook if you need a refresher before completing this exercise.)

1. I feel proud when_____.

2. _____ appreciates me when I help them.

3. I admire _____ because _____.

4. My family says I am good at _____.

5. My friends like that I _____.

6. A compliment I received was_____.

7. The best feedback a teacher ever gave me was _____.

8. My favorite part of my body is _____.

9. I feel good about myself when_____.

10. I have the most fun _____.

11. When I _____, I am so engaged I lose track of time.

12. A memory that makes me happy is _____.

13. My friends rely on me to _____.

14. I am helpful to others when_____.

15. I am successful at_____.

SOCIAL COMPARISON

· · · · · ·

"Comparison is the thief of joy."

– Brené Brown

One of the things that teens do very often is compare themselves to others. While this is natural – you are still learning who and how you want to be in the world, and fitting in often seems like a really important priority – comparisons can actually make you feel worse. When we think of people as "better" or "worse" than ourselves, we are engaging in comparison, and often we see ourselves as "less than." In this activity, you will be encouraged to let go of making comparisons by reframing these comparisons as different, but not better.

Two artists (singers/actors/musicians/etc.) who I think are both talented are:

1. _____

2. _____

How are these two artists different from each other? Do they have talents that are unique from one another? Is one clearly better than the other or are you able to view them as just different and both valuable?

_____

_____

_____

Two people I love are:

1. _____

2. _____

How is your love for each of these people different? Do you feel that you love one person more or better than the other, or is it possible that your love for each person can be different but no less important?

_____

_____

_____

When is a time that you felt like you were being compared to someone else? Perhaps a parent comparing you to a sibling? A teacher comparing you to another student? Or a friend comparing you to another friend?

_____

_____

_____

How did you feel in this situation?

_____

_____

_____

When you felt like you were being compared to someone else, how did this help or hurt your ability to be successful in that situation?

_____

_____

_____

When was a time that you compared yourself to someone else? Maybe you compared your life to what you saw on someone's social media posts. Or maybe you compared your body to an image you saw in a magazine. Or maybe you compared your performance in school or sports to that of another individual.

_____

_____

_____

How did you feel in this situation?

_____

_____

_____

How did comparing yourself with that other person help or hurt your ability to be successful in that situation?

_____

_____

_____

CRITICS VS. THE INNER CIRCLE

• • • • • •

In a world of social media and "likes," it is easy to feel like everyone you encounter not only has an opinion about you, but most will not hesitate to share that opinion. While sometimes this can feel good, such as when you get many "likes" and positive comments about a picture of yourself that you posted, it can also leave us very vulnerable to feeling badly about ourselves when we receive negative feedback. We may also end up feeling badly even when we just don't get a lot of feedback at all.

The following worksheet will help you to consider whose opinions you think matter most, and how you want to deal with the opinions of those who you decide are less important.

Most people only have a very small list of people (maybe two or three) who have earned the right to be in their inner circle. People in your inner circle are those who:

- Love you for your strengths *and* for your struggles
- You can be yourself around
- You know have your back, regardless of the situation
- You can have a disagreement or conflict with and still be able to work through things

Because people in your inner circle know the good, the bad, and the ugly – and love you anyway – these are usually the people whose feedback matters most. These people can often help you to see the positive about yourself when you're having a hard time doing so. They also provide a secure sense of knowing that you're cared about and that you matter, regardless of the situation or circumstance.

Critics, on the other hand, are all the other people in the world who do not hesitate to share their critiques and judgments. These people have **not** earned the right to be in your inner circle. Therefore, it is up to you to decide how you want to respond to their unsolicited feedback, if at all!

MY INNER CIRCLE

· · · · · ·

Who are the people in your inner circle?

_____

_____

_____

Over the next week, take a survey of the people in your inner circle by asking them the following questions and writing down their responses:

What do you think are my strengths?

_____

_____

_____

What do you think I need to work on improving?

_____

_____

_____

After you collect this feedback from everyone in your inner circle, respond to these reflection questions:

What did my inner circle tell me that makes me feel loved, cared for, appreciated, or valued?

_____

_____

_____

What was surprising about the feedback?

_____

_____

_____

Do you agree with your inner circle's input on your areas for improvement? Why or why not?

_____

_____

_____

Moving forward, how will you choose to respond to feedback (positive or negative) from your inner circle?

_____

_____

_____

In the future, how will you choose to respond to feedback (positive or negative) from those who are NOT in your inner circle (your critics)?

_____

_____

_____

POSITIVE SELF-AFFIRMATIONS

· · · · · ·

One of the ways that we can increase our self-esteem is to remind ourselves of positive things. As we develop the habit of seeing positivity, gratitude, or a strength in ourselves, we help ourselves to start believing this. Sometimes people refer to this as "fake it 'til you make it" – which really means that we often have to practice more positive ideas and beliefs to really make them a part of our understanding. (This is similar to what you did with reframing and comparison.)

Below, is a list of positive self-affirmations. Look through them and see which ones you think are true about yourself. If you have a hard time believing any of them, pick ones that seem as if you could possibly imagine them being true. (Chances are, they are already true!)

Each day for the next week, select one positive affirmation. In the morning, say the affirmation out loud at least five times. Throughout the day, repeat this affirmation to yourself in your head, out loud, and write it down. Try to keep the affirmation in your mind all day long. **Use the worksheet on the next two pages to record your daily self-affirmation practice**.

You are strong.
You are enough.
You do not need to prove yourself to anyone.
You do not need to be perfect.
Everyone struggles and makes mistakes. In this way, you are just like everyone else.
You are loved.
I accept myself.
I love myself.
You can do anything you put your mind to.
You are getting better every day.
You can make things happen.
I trust myself to make good decisions.
You are full of energy.
You deserve the best.
You are peaceful and calm.
I radiate positive energy.
You are a survivor.
You are in control of your life.
I see potential in myself and my future.
I treat myself with love and respect.
I know that every problem has a solution.
You deserve to be happy.
You are worth it.

DAILY POSITIVE SELF–AFFIRMATIONS PRACTICE

· · · · · ·

Record your daily self-affirmations practice here.

Day 1 Date: _____

Positive self-affirmation of the day:

_____

Day 2 Date: _____

Positive self-affirmation of the day:

_____

Day 3 Date: _____

Positive self-affirmation of the day:

_____

Day 4 Date: _____

Positive self-affirmation of the day:

_____

Day 5 Date: _____

Positive self-affirmation of the day:

_____

Day 6 Date: _____

Positive self-affirmation of the day:

_____

Day 7 Date: _____

Positive self-affirmation of the day:

_____

SELF-AFFIRMATIONS PRACTICE REFLECTION

· · · · · ·

At the end of your week, answer these questions by circling the number that best corresponds with your response:

1. I practiced my self-affirmations daily:

    1 – Never

    2 – Rarely

    3 – Sometimes

    4 – Often

    5 – Always

2. Practicing my self-affirmations was:

    1 – Very difficult

    2 – Difficult

    3 – Neutral

    4 – Easy

    5 – Very easy

3. After practicing my self-affirmations for one week, I feel:

    1 – Much worse

    2 – Somewhat worse

    3 – About the same

    4 – Somewhat better

    5 – Much better

Total score = _____

*Note your total score for these three questions. If it is not as high as you would like it to be, try this activity again and see if your score increases.

DAILY SELF-AFFIRMATION REMINDERS

· · · · · ·

The purpose of this activity is to find ways to remind yourself of your positive self-affirmations throughout the day and week. **Use the following notes or get a pad of sticky notes to create your own positive affirmation reminders.**

Once you have a bunch of reminders, place them around your home (or you can ask a parent or family member to hide them for you). You can hang them on a door or mirror, put them inside of a book or notebook, stick one by your toothbrush, or stick one inside of your favorite cereal box—anywhere you are likely to look at least once in the next week.

As you go about your daily routines, you will encounter your notes. Each time you do, take a moment to really let your message to yourself sink in and to notice how it feels when you give yourself kind messages.

I am in control of my own thoughts feelings, and behaviors.

Judging Yourself

I am already enough.

Smile— it's contagious!

I deserve the best.

Don't forget to love yourself.

IDENTIFYING VALUES

• • • • • •

We all have a series of beliefs about what matters to us. We make choices and decisions based on these values. Identifying our core values helps us decide where we want to focus more or less of our time and attention. Sometimes, when we take an objective look at our values, we are surprised to find how much (or how little) we are living our values.

From the following list, check off all of the values that are most important to you. Then, go back a second time and identify your top five values. You will use these in the next exercise as well.

_____ Family		_____ Friendship
_____ Love		_____ Happiness
_____ Wealth		_____ Success
_____ Freedom		_____ Fun
_____ Power		_____ Independence
_____ Knowledge		_____ Honesty
_____ Humor		_____ Loyalty
_____ Popularity		_____ Fairness
_____ Relaxation		_____ Responsibility
_____ Adventure		_____ Achievement
_____ Stability		_____ Variety
_____ Safety		_____ Recognition
_____ Calm		_____ Nature

MAPPING YOUR VALUES

· · · · · ·

Imagine a pie chart, where different parts of the "pie" represent different amounts. **Using your top five values, color in the circle with the time and energy you spend on each of your top five values now.** (It may be easier to use five different colors for this.)

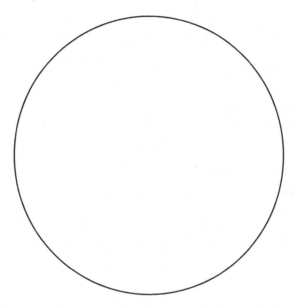

Now color in the circle with the time and energy you **would like** to spend on your top five values.

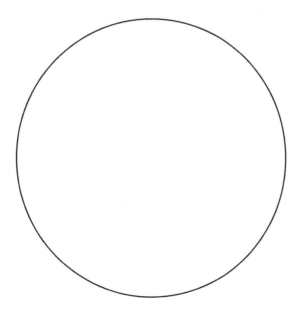

REFLECTING ON YOUR VALUES

· · · · · ·

1. As you completed the previous exercise (filling in the pie chart) what did you observe about your values? How much are you currently living your values compared to how much you would like to live your values?

_____

_____

_____

2. What are some areas that you might like to change to spend *more* time living your values? Are there any areas that you want to spend *less* time with?

_____

_____

_____

3. What are some things that you might try that would help you feel more connected to your values and put them into practice?

_____

_____

_____

THINKING ABOUT VALUES

· · · · · ·

Once we have identified our core values, there's still work to do. Values aren't necessarily static over time – our priorities, knowledge, and experiences shift. **Here are some questions for you to consider. Take 5–10 minutes per question to write your answers.**

1. Values are personal and unique to you. What are some *similarities* in values, as well as *differences* in values, between you and your *parents*? What are some *similarities* and *differences* in values between you and your *friends*?

_____

_____

_____

_____

_____

2. Bring to mind someone you admire (this can be someone you know or a public figure). What values do you think are important to this person? What might be similar or different from your values?

_____

_____

_____

3. Think about someone you really *don't* like or admire. What values do you think are important to them? What might be similar or different from your values?

_____

_____

_____

4. What values do you currently have that may have changed over time? What experiences have you had that influenced this shift in your values?

_____

_____

_____

5. What values from the "Identifying Values" worksheet do you think may become important to you in the future? What values do you imagine may be less important to you in the future than they are now?

_____

_____

_____

SETTING GOALS

• • • • • •

Regardless of your age, it can be helpful to think in terms of the goals that you have for yourself and your life.

Goals are important for a number of reasons:

1. Goals help you focus your time and energy on what really matters.

2. Goals help you measure progress and increase your confidence when you see successes, however small.

3. Goals help you avoid distraction and procrastination.

4. Goals give you motivation.

5. Goals help you see the big picture.

In order to help you better visualize your goals, complete the "Mapping My Life" activity on the following page, which asks you to imagine what your ideal life would look like in one month, one year, and even 10 years from now.

When filling out the chart, make sure to include various aspects of your life, including family, friends, school/career, and health/wellness. There is also room at the bottom of the page for any other goals that you may have for yourself and your life.

For now, you do not need to worry about how you will get there (or if it even seems possible), but just focus on where you want to go. Be as specific as possible!

MAPPING MY LIFE

· · · · · ·

	One month from now…	One year from now…	10 years from now…
Family			
Friends			
School/Career			
Health/Wellness			
Other			

ARE YOU READY TO CHANGE?

• • • • • •

What is one thing in your life that causes problems or that you (or others) would like to see you change?

_____

How important is it for you to change?

1	2	3	4	5	6	7	8	9	10
Not at all important									Extremely important

Using the following scale, how ready you are to change?

1	2	3	4	5	6	7	8	9	10
Not prepared to change									Already changing

If you answered 1–3 on either of these questions, what would need to happen for you to consider making this change in the future?

_____

_____

If you answered 4–6 on either of these questions, what might your next steps towards change be?

_____

_____

If you answered 7–10 on either of these questions, what action steps will help you to be successful in changing?

_____

_____

SMART GOALS

· · · · · ·

When you want to make a change and set goals for yourself, there are a few things you can do to increase your chances of successfully meeting those goals. A simple thing to remember is to make sure your goals are **SMART**:

S	Specific	With clearly defined actions
M	Measurable	With a way to measure progress and success
A	Attainable	Achievable and realistic
R	Relevant	Important to you based on your values
T	Time-bound	Within a clear timeframe

Let's say that you are interested in being healthier. While this is a great thing to shoot for, this is not a SMART goal. What do you mean by healthier? How will you know when you have reached this goal? How does it fit with your current diet and exercise habits? Why is it important to you? How long will it take?

We can take your interest in being healthier and turn it into a smart goal by identifying the SMART components:

S	Specific	I will be healthier by eating more fruits and vegetables and by increasing my exercise.
M	Measurable	I will eat at least five fruits and vegetables every day, and I will exercise at least 20 minutes, at least three days per week.
A	Attainable	I already know what to eat and try to have fruits and vegetables at least once a day, so this goal is attainable.
R	Relevant	I believe that having a healthy body will help me manage my emotions, so this goal is relevant.
T	Time-bound	I will track my fruits, vegetables, and exercise for one month.

Practice setting SMART Goals on the next page.

SETTING A SMART GOAL

· · · · · ·

What is one area of your life in which you are interested in making a change or working towards a goal?

_____

Now, take this goal and make it SMART:

S	Specific	*What specific actions will you take towards this goal?*
M	Measurable	*How will you measure success?*
A	Attainable	*How realistic and achievable is this goal?*
R	Relevant	*Why does this goal matter to you?*
T	Time-bound	*What is the time frame for achieving this goal?*

SETTING YOURSELF UP FOR SUCCESS

· · · · · ·

Once you have a SMART goal, you need to set yourself up for success by making sure that you have a plan for when things are going well and also for when you hit the inevitable bumps in the road.

What is your main reason for wanting to reach this goal? Why is it so important to you?

_____

_____

_____

_____

Close your eyes and imagine that you have reached your goal. Describe in as much detail how you will feel. What will be different in your life?

_____

_____

_____

_____

Next, close your eyes and imagine the barriers that might get in the way of you achieving your goal. Be as specific as you can, and really try to imagine yourself experiencing these barriers and then finding ways to overcome them. Describe the barriers in as much detail as you can. Describe how you see yourself overcoming these barriers as well.

_____

_____

_____

_____

For each barrier or challenge, what can you do to improve your chances of success?

1. _____

2. _____

3. _____

What personal strengths do you have that will help you to reach this goal?

1. _____

2. _____

3. _____

As a last step, take a moment to think about how you will celebrate your success. Write down at least one way that you will celebrate when you reach your goal.

1. _____

2. _____

COMMITTING TO MY GOAL

· · · · · ·

Research has shown that people are most likely to commit to – and, in turn, achieve – a goal when:

1. Their goal is consistent with their values.

2. They commit to specific behaviors that will help them reach their goal.

This activity will help you to make sure you are ready to commit to your goal by ensuring that it aligns with your values and by helping you identify concrete behaviors you can take to reach this goal.

My goal:

_____

This goal reflects the following personal values:

1. _____

2. _____

Now, think about the specific behaviors you would need to do to achieve this goal. What are some small steps you could take to reach your goal? Right now, don't worry about whether or not you want to take these steps or believe that you can take these steps. Just focus on behaviors that you could do on a regular basis to help you reach your goal.

1. _____

2. _____

3. _____

4. _____

5. _____

6. _____

For each behavior that you listed, how committed are you to actually doing this behavior on a regular basis to help you work towards your goal?

#1: _____

1	2	3	4	5
Not at all committed		Neutral		Completely committed

#2: _____

1	2	3	4	5
Not at all committed		Neutral		Completely committed

#3: _____

1	2	3	4	5
Not at all committed		Neutral		Completely committed

#4: _____

1	2	3	4	5
Not at all committed		Neutral		Completely committed

#5: _____

1	2	3	4	5
Not at all committed		Neutral		Completely committed

#6: _____

1	2	3	4	5
Not at all committed		Neutral		Completely committed

Based on your answers, select one behavior that you are ready to implement now to help

you achieve your goal: _____

GOAL MILESTONES

• • • • • •

Long-term goals, by definition, take a long time to complete. One way to tackle these goals is to set short-term milestones that you can track along the way to your long-term goal. Working towards short-term milestones will also help you to see your successes and feel motivated!

This worksheet is intended to help you break down your long-term goal into short-term milestones and to track your progress.

Long-term goal:

_____

Short-term milestone: _____

Date to achieve: _____

Short-term milestone: _____

Date to achieve: _____

Short-term milestone: _____

Date to achieve: _____

Short-term milestone: _____

Date to achieve: _____

8

SAFETY

One of the core ways that trauma impacts individuals is by impacting their perception of safety and security (NCTSN, 2012). Not only does trauma change the physiology of the brain in such a way that it is predisposed to respond with a fight, flight, or freeze response (Bremner, 2006), but it can also lead to changes in our core life assumptions, such that we begin to view the world as unsafe and other people as dangerous (Janoff-Bulman, 1992). **In these ways, trauma can lead to hypervigilance and a focus on protecting ourselves.** For example, a teenager who has experienced an assault by an adult male may generalize their fear to adult males in general. In turn, that teen will be uncomfortable in everyday situations involving male figures, which can impact their ability to complete schoolwork, or work with a teacher or coach. Similarly, a teen who has experienced trauma outside of the home may become increasingly fearful of leaving the house, even to attend events with their parents or trusted adults.

Paradoxically, trauma can also lead some individuals to engage in unnecessarily high-risk behaviors (NCTSN, 2012). For teenagers, this is particularly relevant, as adolescents are already likely to engage in risk-taking behaviors in the course of their normal development. This propensity toward risk-taking behavior is, at least in part, due to the fact that the adolescent prefrontal cortex – which is responsible for planning, decision making, and inhibiting impulses – is not yet fully developed (Casey, Getz, & Galvan, 2008). Some risk-taking behaviors are influenced by a desire to fit in socially with peers, and social norms can also greatly impact what behaviors teenagers perceive as risky. For example, certain behaviors – such as "sexting" (sending sexually provocative text messages or images) and "cyberbullying" (bullying others via social media) – have become alarmingly commonplace to the extent that many teens do not perceive these behaviors as inherently risky.

Importantly, trauma further exacerbates this already normative adolescent tendency to engage in impulsive and risky behavior by affecting adolescents' emotional reactivity. Trauma can result in emotional *hypo*-reactivity, causing teens to exhibit potential increases in sensation-seeking behavior as a means of combatting a sense of emotional numbness. Alternatively, adolescents who have experienced trauma may experience emotional *hyper*-reactivity, causing them to respond more strongly and more quickly to potential stressors. As a result of this emotional activation, they are more vulnerable to engaging in excessive risk-taking behaviors. Indeed, youth who have experienced abuse are at higher risk for truancy, running away, and homelessness, and they have a 53% higher risk for juvenile arrest than their non-abused peers (NASMHPD & NTAC, 2004).

This excessive risk-taking behavior puts adolescents at risk for numerous negative outcomes, including teen pregnancy, substance abuse, legal problems, school drop-out, violence, injury, and sometimes even death (IM & NRC, 2011). Teens who have experienced trauma are also at greater risk for suicidal and self-harm behavior (Flannery, Singer, & Wester, 2001), as they often engage in such behaviors as a means of distracting themselves from negative feelings or punishing themselves.

In addition, individuals who have experienced childhood trauma are at increased risk for future victimization. This may be, at least in part, due to the fact that exposure to trauma can make it more difficult for individuals to distinguish between safe and unsafe situations, which influences their own self-protective and risk-taking behaviors (NCTSN, 2012). For example, females who have experienced trauma are at higher risk for *future* sexual assault (NASMHPD & NTAC, 2004). In a similar fashion, adolescents who have been exposed to interpersonal violence show an increased risk for substance use and abuse (Kilpatrick et al., 2000).

However, it is important to remember that risk-taking behaviors are not inherently bad. Some level of risk-taking is an important part of the developmental tasks of adolescence. Risk-taking motivates teens to become more independent, to try new things, and to figure out who they are and where they are going (IM & NRC, 2011). In this respect, some risk-taking can lead to positive outcomes, including increased civic engagement and social change, as well as creativity and innovation. Therefore, when considering safety concerns, it is important to consider normal adolescent development, as well as the impact of trauma on this developmental trajectory. Trauma can contribute to the development of risk-taking behaviors (and, in turn, lead to safety issues), but safety issues can develop in adolescents regardless of their history of trauma or adversity.

HOW TO IMPLEMENT THE SAFETY WORKSHEETS

The activities in this section target risk-taking behaviors in general, and they also cover some common safety concerns that may develop in the wake of trauma, including self-harm, alcohol and substance use, suicidal thoughts and/or behaviors, and risky sexual behavior. These worksheets are not intended to take the place of formalized treatment for substance abuse, suicidality, or self-harm. Evidence-based models of treatment for these problems are available and should be accessed in any case where the adolescent client is struggling with significant symptoms of this nature. Rather, the exercises in this workbook are designed to help the clinician assess any areas of potential concern, educate the adolescent regarding safety and making safer choices, and provide interventions for teens who may be exhibiting some mild to moderate symptoms in any of these areas.

Self-Harm: Although self-harm behaviors are most common among individuals who have experienced trauma, especially those who have survived sexual trauma (Gibson & Crenshaw, 2015), these behaviors are relatively common among adolescents in general. For example, an estimated 17% of teens report that they have engaged in at least one self-harm behavior in their lifetime (Muehlenkamp, Claes, Havertape, & Plener, 2012). Therefore, the cultural and peer context may play at least some role in the development of self-harm behaviors during adolescence.

Self-harm behaviors can only be effectively treated and managed when they are properly assessed. This is complicated by the fact that many teenagers will conceal their self-harm. The activities in this section are intended to help the clinician assess the adolescent's risk for and engagement in self-harm behaviors. For those who are identified as engaging in self-harm, there are also some basic activities included to explore the teen's motivation for self-harm behaviors, as well as their readiness to change these behaviors.

Alcohol and Substance Use: Numerous studies have demonstrated the link between trauma exposure and substance abuse among adolescents. For example, teens who have experienced trauma are more likely to use substances, perhaps as a means of self-medicating or managing their symptoms. Similarly, teens who use substances are at higher risk of being victimized, in part because they are more likely to put themselves into unsafe situations in the context of their substance use (NCTSN, 2008).

The exercises in this section are intended to help the clinician assess to what extent the adolescent may be using substances, as well as their motivation and willingness to change these behaviors. In the event that a pattern of substance abuse is identified, it is recommended that the clinician utilize evidence-based treatment methods for the treatment of addiction or substance abuse, the content of which is beyond the scope of this workbook.

Suicidal Thoughts and Behaviors: Research demonstrates that children who have experienced trauma are at a much higher risk for suicidal thoughts and behaviors than their non-traumatized peers (Salzinger, Rosario, Feldman, & Ng-Mak, 2007). In fact, some studies have shown that as many as 30% of individuals who have experienced certain types of childhood trauma will attempt suicide (Fergusson, Horwood, & Lynskey, 1996).

Treatment of significant suicidal behavior goes beyond the scope of this workbook, and the exercises contained within should not be considered a substitute for a thorough suicide risk assessment and response. However, the prevalence of suicidality among adolescents who have experienced trauma suggests that many teens in treatment for trauma will experience at least some suicidal thoughts (Shain, 2016). Therefore, this workbook includes a template for adolescents to develop a plan for keeping themselves safe in the event that they may have unsafe thoughts. This template may be used for adolescents who endorse having had some suicidal thoughts or as a preemptive precaution for those who may not endorse suicidal thoughts but exhibit other risk factors for developing those thoughts, such as depression or hopelessness.

Risky Sexual Behavior: Adolescence is a time when individuals are developing their knowledge about sexuality and their identity as a sexual being, and when sexual behaviors often increase. Sexual development, like all other elements of human development, involves physical, cognitive, emotional, social, and moral maturation processes. Because trauma impacts adolescent development in various ways, it can thus have a significant impact on the sexual choices of adolescents. Moreover, research has shown that exposure to any type of trauma in childhood – not just sexual trauma – is associated with an increased risk for risky sexual behaviors (Thompson et al., 2017).

Regardless of whether or not a teen is currently sexually active, they can benefit from having accurate information about sexual health and sexual well-being. Furthermore, despite the common misconception that sex education may promote teens to engage in sexual activity, evidence suggests that the opposite is true. Adolescents who are well-informed tend to delay the onset of sexual activity, and they also exhibit the skills to make safer decisions regarding their sexual behavior.

MAKING SAFE CHOICES

Explain to clients that it is important to talk about safety and what that means in their life. Sometimes, people have different definitions or ideas about what is "safe." For example, one of their friends may think it's safe to drink alcohol and use drugs, but another friend may think that's not safe (but may be willing to engage in unprotected sex). Sometimes, teenagers will regularly engage in behaviors that are potentially unsafe, but they don't think it's a problem.

Reiterate to clients that therapy is meant to be a "safe place" – meaning that it's a place where they can talk honestly and openly about their thoughts, feelings, and behaviors. Help them understand that when they are honest with you, you can support them in making the best choices. Use the worksheet on the following page to help clients start talking about safety.

SAFETY: TAKING STOCK

• • • • • •

In order to start talking about safety, fill out the following chart to indicate any behaviors you have ever done – even if you only engaged in the behavior once or if it is not a problem for you. Remember that this worksheet is part of the process for talking openly and honestly.

	Age when I first tried it:	Last time I did it:	How many times I do it per week:	This is a problem for me (yes/no):
Drinking alcohol				
Using drugs				
Smoking cigarettes				
Having unprotected sex				
Thinking about suicide				
Cutting or burning myself				
Breaking the law				
Other unsafe behaviors:				

NUMBING

· · · · · ·

One way that many people try to manage their strong feelings is through numbing behaviors. Numbing behaviors are any behaviors that you do that may help you feel better in the short term but that hurt you in the long term. They keep you from achieving your goals and living the life you wish to have. When you try to numb negative feelings, you end up numbing any positive feelings as well. Therefore, numbing behaviors keep you from fully experiencing positive emotions, such as happiness, love, and joy.

Look at the following list of numbing behaviors and circle any that you use. You can also add any other numbing behaviors to the list.

Overeating	Spending too much money	Gossiping
Using alcohol or drugs	Wasting time online	Oversleeping
Smoking	Excessively playing video games	Self-harm
Isolating from others	Other:	Other:

Replacing Numbing with Self-Care

Whereas numbing behaviors help us feel better in the short term, self-care behaviors are choices we make that truly nourish our souls and help us towards our long-term goals. These behaviors not only help us in the moment, but they also help us to feel rejuvenated, positive, and comforted. They improve our mental, physical, and emotional health. Self-care strategies can include going for a walk, doing some breathing, taking a bath, calling a friend, or playing with a pet. Additional self-care ideas are provided in Chapter 4 (see "Healthy Coping Activities" on pages 90-91).

What are two self-care strategies that you are willing to try as an alternative to numbing behaviors? If you need a reminder, refer back to Chapter 4 for ideas.

1. _____

2. _____

IS IT WORTH THE RISK?

A *risk* is any situation in which there could be possible exposure to harm, danger, or a negative outcome. Often, adults warn adolescents to be careful about taking too many risks, as they can be dangerous. Some examples of dangerous risks include: drinking, using drugs, driving too fast, or engaging in certain sexual and online behaviors.

While people sometimes think that all risk-taking behaviors are bad, this is not true. Taking risks is a normal part of being a teenager. It is a way that teens grow and learn about who they are. Examples of some positive risks include: making new friends, trying a new hobby, or experimenting with new fashions.

So, how do your clients know if a risk is worth taking or not? One important question to ask themselves is: "How dangerous could this be?" It is important to remember that no possible payoff of risky behavior is worth risking death!

IS IT WORTH THE RISK?

• • • • • •

Look at the following list of risky behaviors. "X" out any behaviors that could pose a risk of death. For any behaviors that do not pose a risk of death, use the rating scale to indicate how risky you believe each choice might be.

	1 **Positive outcome more likely than negative outcome**	2	3 **Positive or negative outcome equally likely**	4	5 **Negative outcome more likely than positive outcome**
Drinking alcohol					
Hitchhiking					
Cheating on a test					
Riding in a car with someone who is drunk or high					
Trying out for a school sports team or play					
Smoking marijuana					
Sitting at lunch with a student who is new to the school					
Skipping school					
Meeting an online stranger in person					

A SAFE NIGHT OUT

. . . . . .

One way that you can decrease the likelihood of a negative outcome is by *thinking ahead of time* about the ways that you can keep yourself safe in a potentially risky situation.

Let's imagine that you are planning to attend a party with some kids that you know from school. The party is at the home of an acquaintance that you know, but you have never been there before. The party is being held on a Saturday evening.

Using the following boxes, list some things that you can do to help keep yourself safe in this situation:

Before you go:	**While you are there:**
On the way home:	**In case of an emergency:**

TAKING CHARGE OF MY SAFETY

· · · · · ·

What triggers my unsafe thoughts or behaviors:

_____

_____

_____

The unsafe thoughts or behaviors that I have most often:

_____

_____

_____

Ways I can distract myself when I am feeling unsafe:

_____

_____

_____

_____

People I can talk to when I am feeling unsafe:

_____

_____

_____

_____

Save these phone #s in your phone for easy access!

In case of emergency, I can call:

_____

_____

_____

_____

Call 911 for life-threatening emergencies. Your therapist can provide you with #s for crisis hotlines or other emergency services.

Coping strategies I can use:

_____

_____

_____

_____

STAGES OF CHANGE

· · · · · ·

When people are considering making a change in their life, there is a natural series of steps that they progress through on the path to making that change, which is sometimes referred to as the Stages of Change. **These stages can be applied to almost any change you are trying to make in your life.**

Precontemplation

Don't see the behavior as a problem

Don't recognize the potential costs or negative consequences of the behavior

May have tried to change before but have "given up"

Contemplation

Mixed feelings about changing

Can see some benefits to changing, but also hesitant to make the changes

Preparation

Have decided to make a change

Thinking about the steps necessary to make that change

Beginning to make minor changes in behavior

Action

Taking significant actions to change

Starting to make progress towards the goal

Maintenance and Relapse Prevention

Maintaining the change on a long-term basis

Able to maintain progress despite challenges

Planning to avoid relapse

HARD CHOICES: MAKING CHANGES AND WORKING TOWARDS GOALS

• • • • • •

Before you commit to making a change or working towards a goal, it can be helpful to consider whether this change is right for you. You have been thinking about safety and what behaviors are potentially safe/unsafe. Sometimes, the choices that we make have an impact that we didn't intend, such as causing problems in our relationships, negatively affecting our health, or creating financial difficulties. For example, choosing to drink and drive can result in many of these negative consequences.

Of course, certain choices can also result in positive consequences. It's helpful to think about the various aspects of your life that might improve (or get more difficult) if you make a decision to change your behavior.

First, think of a "positive" or "safe" behavior. Use the following chart to evaluate how making a change to do more of this behavior will impact your health/wellness, family relationships, social relationships, and school/career. Use the "+" side of the chart to identify all of the reasons why change would be good for you, as well as all the reasons why you want to change. Use the "–" side of the chart to identify any reasons why you are reluctant to change or reasons why the change might not be good for you.

School/Career

Family/Relationships

_____ | _____

_____ | _____

_____ | _____

_____ | _____

Social Relationships

_____ | _____

_____ | _____

_____ | _____

_____ | _____

Health/Wellness

_____ | _____

_____ | _____

_____ | _____

_____ | _____

Then, think of a "negative" or "unsafe" behavior. Use the following chart to evaluate how making a change to do less of this behavior will impact your health/wellness, family relationships, social relationships, and school/career. Use the "+" side of the chart to identify all of the reasons why change would be good for you, as well as all the reasons why you want to change. Use the "−" side of the chart to identify any reasons why you are reluctant to change or reasons why the change might not be good for you.

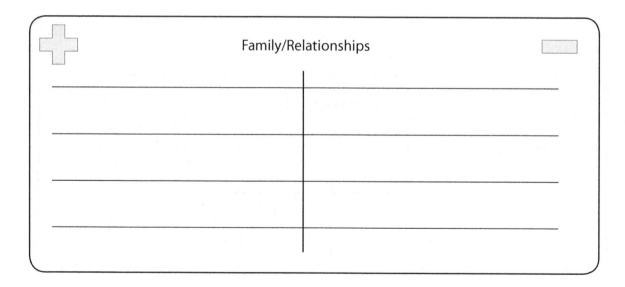

Social Relationships

_____

_____

_____

_____

Health/Wellness

_____

_____

_____

WEIGHING YOUR OPTIONS: SUBSTANCE USE

· · · · · ·

Deciding whether or not to change your substance use is a tough choice. This exercise will help you to consider why you may or may not want to change your alcohol or substance use.

Use the following chart to evaluate how changing your use will impact your health/ wellness, family relationships, social relationships, and school/career. Use the "+" side of the chart to identify all of the reasons why changing your use would be good for you and all the reasons why you want to change. Use the "−" side of the chart to identify any reasons why you are reluctant to change your use or reasons why the change might not be good for you.

+	School/Career	−

+	Family/Relationships	−

Social Relationships

_____ | _____

_____ | _____

_____ | _____

_____ | _____

Health/Wellness

_____ | _____

_____ | _____

_____ | _____

_____ | _____

ARE YOU READY TO CHANGE
YOUR SUBSTANCE USE?

• • • • • •

How important is it for you to change your substance use?

1	2	3	4	5	6	7	8	9	10
Not at all important									Extremely important

Using the following scale, how ready are you to change your substance use?

1	2	3	4	5	6	7	8	9	10
Not prepared to change									Already changing

If you answered 1–3 on either of these questions, what would need to happen for you to consider making this change in the future?

_____

_____

If you answered 4–6 on either of these questions, what might your next steps toward change be?

_____

_____

If you answered 7–10 on either these questions, what action steps will help you to be successful in changing?

_____

_____

SELF-HARM

· · · · · ·

Self-harm involves intentionally hurting yourself in any way in order to relieve emotional pain or distress. People may self-harm in only one way, but more often they engage in multiple forms of self-harm.

Some of the ways that teenagers may self-harm are listed in the following chart. **Use the chart to indicate how frequently you engage in any of these forms of self-harm.** There is also space at the bottom to add any others that you might think of.

Self-Harm Behaviors:	Never	Rarely	Sometimes	Very Often	Always
Cutting myself					
Burning myself					
Scratching my skin					
Punching hard objects					
Banging my head against something hard					
Pinching or bruising myself					
Pulling my hair					
Other:					
Other:					
Other:					

WEIGHING YOUR OPTIONS: SELF-HARM

· · · · · ·

When people self-harm, it is usually for good reason. Deciding to stop or decrease your self-harming behaviors is not an easy choice.

Use the following chart to evaluate how stopping or decreasing your self-harm will impact your health/wellness, family relationships, social relationships, and school/ career. Use the "+" side of the chart to identify all of the reasons why stopping or decreasing your self-harm would be good for you, as well as all the reasons why you want to make the change. Use the "–" side of the chart to identify any reasons why you are reluctant to stop or decrease your self-harm behavior or reasons why doing so might not be helpful.

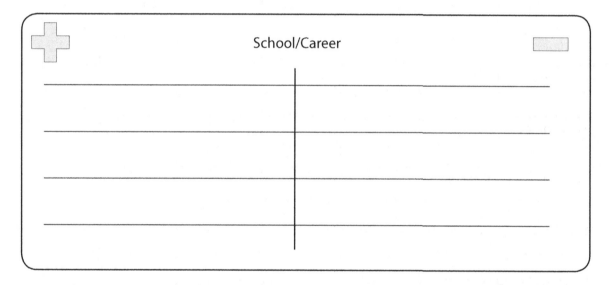

School/Career

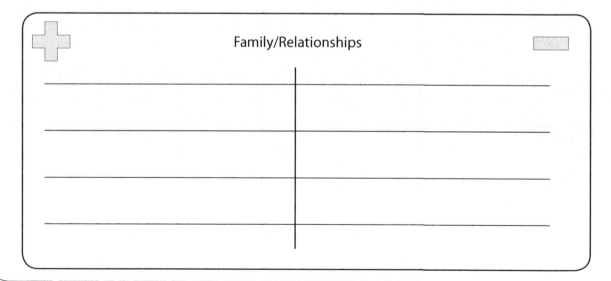

Family/Relationships

Social Relationships

_____|_____

_____|_____

_____|_____

_____|_____

Health/Wellness

_____|_____

_____|_____

_____|_____

_____|_____

ARE YOU READY TO STOP SELF-HARMING?

• • • • • •

How important is it for you to stop or decrease your self-harm behaviors?

1	2	3	4	5	6	7	8	9	10
Not at all important									Extremely important

Using the following scale, how ready are you to stop or decrease your self-harm behaviors?

1	2	3	4	5	6	7	8	9	10
Not prepared to change									Already changing

If you answered 1–3 on either of these questions, what would need to happen for you to consider making this change in the future?

_____

_____

If you answered 4–6 on either of these questions, what might your next steps towards change be?

_____

_____

If you answered 7–10 on either these questions, what action steps will help you to be successful in changing?

_____

_____

WORKING TOGETHER TO MANAGE SUICIDAL THOUGHTS

• • • • • •

Thoughts about suicide are not that uncommon in teenagers, especially those who are struggling with symptoms of depression and those who have experienced trauma.

Talking about these thoughts can be scary, or you may worry about what others might think if you admit to having these thoughts. However, sharing your thoughts with your therapist is an important first step in getting the help that you need to manage these thoughts. **This activity will help you to share your thoughts about suicide with your therapist so he or she can help you better**.

Do you ever wish you were not alive? Or that you would fall asleep and never wake up? What thoughts like this have you had?

_____

_____

_____

Do you ever have thoughts about killing yourself? Write down those thoughts:

_____

_____

_____

When you think about killing yourself, do you ever think about how you would do it? Write down your thoughts here:

_____

_____

_____

Have you ever tried to kill yourself? Or started to try to kill yourself? Or prepared for your death in any other way?

_____

_____

_____

What is your one most important reason for wanting to be alive?

_____

_____

_____

MY BODY, MY CHOICES

· · · · · ·

Making decisions about your sexuality and sexual behavior are complex, and ultimately you are the only person who can decide what is right for you and under what circumstances.

Here are some questions to help you think about the choices you make with regard to your body and your sexuality.

Most of my friends share these values about sex:

_____

_____

_____

Values

My family's values regarding sex include:

_____

_____

_____

I learned about my body and sexuality from:

_____

_____

Knowledge

If I have questions about my body or sex, I can ask:

_____

_____

_____

I feel that sex is right for me in the following circumstances:

_____

_____

Choices

The kind of sexual relationship that is right for me is:

_____

_____

_____

TALKING ABOUT SEX

· · · · · ·

You are in charge of your body, your behaviors, and your choices. In order to make sure that others respect your boundaries, it is important for you to be able to communicate in a clear, assertive manner. **For each of the following situations, how could you respond in a way that is assertive and clear? Write down an example of what you might say**.

1. Your partner leans in to kiss you, but you do not want them to.

_____

_____

2. You want to tell your best friend that you are gay.

_____

_____

3. Your partner asks you to have sex with them, but you do not want to.

_____

_____

4. You want your partner to use a condom.

_____

_____

5. You want to break up with your partner.

_____

_____

6. You need to tell your partner that you have an STD.

_____

_____

WISHING YOU HAPPINESS
ALONG YOUR JOURNEY
Handout for Teens

• • • • • •

Congratulations! You've done a lot of work and built a WHOLE LOT of skills. You have spent time learning and understanding your emotions, and the way your thoughts, feelings, and behaviors are connected. By learning specific thinking skills, you've been able to separate worry and anxiety, and develop new ways to address fears and concerns. You've had a chance to figure out what common triggers or upsetting situations might be and worked out ways you can deal with them in a healthy manner. You've discovered and practiced skills to manage stress and respond differently, as well as to make healthy choices that support your goals. And speaking of goals: You've looked at your strengths and values, and practiced what to do in order to move forward in the ways that you want.

Being positive, taking good care of yourself, making safe choices, and building strong, healthy relationships have also been part of your journey. Congratulations on that one – learning to set boundaries and use assertive communication can be challenging (and many adults still need to work on these areas)!

In the beginning of this workbook, we acknowledged that sometimes life is really hard for a long time. We also started out saying that it is possible to feel better. Hopefully, you've started to feel better and more in control of your life. You can use the exercises in this workbook any time; you don't have to be struggling or going through trauma. Remember that these exercises are geared to help everyone live their best life. Stress will always happen (for everyone), but the goal is to keep building the skills needed to manage stress more easily. Keep in mind that the more you practice these skills, the stronger they will get. (This is the science of neuroplasticity and learning!)

We are so glad you've taken the time to invest in yourself. We wish you many moments of savoring, gratitude, and happiness along your life journey.

Dr. Kristina & Dr. Jill

REFERENCES

For your convenience, purchasers can download and print worksheets and handouts from www.pesi.com/TTTT

American Psychiatric Association. (2013). *Diagnostic and statistical manual of mental disorders* (5th ed.). Arlington, VA: Author.

Association for Behavioral and Cognitive Therapies. (2018). *How do I choose a therapist?* Retrieved from: http://www.abct.org/Help/?m=mFindH elp&fa=HowToChooseTherapist.

Breiding, M. J. (2014). Prevalence and characteristics of sexual violence, stalking, and intimate partner violence victimization—National Intimate Partner and Sexual Violence Survey, United States, 2011. *Morbidity and Mortality Weekly Report Surveillance Summaries, 63*(8), 1–18.

Breiding, M. J., Basile, K. C., Smith, S. G., Black, M. C., & Mahendra, R. R. (2015). *Intimate partner violence surveillance: Uniform definitions and recommended data elements, version 2.0.* Atlanta, GA: National Center for Injury Prevention and Control, Centers for Disease Control and Prevention.

Bremner, J. D. (2006). Traumatic stress: Effects on the brain. *Dialogues in Clinical Neuroscience, 8*(4), 445–461.

Burns, D. (1989). *The feeling good handbook.* New York: HarperCollins.

Casey, B. J., Getz, S., & Galvan, A. (2008). The adolescent brain. *Developmental Review, 28*(1), 62–77.

Cohen, J. A., Mannarino, A. P., & Deblinger, E. (2006). *Treating trauma and traumatic grief in children and adolescents.* New York: Guilford Press.

Cook, A., Spinazzola, J., Ford, J., Lanktree, C., Blaustein, M., Cloitre, ... van der Kolk, B. (2005). Complex trauma in children and adolescents. *Psychiatric Annals, 35,* 390–398.

Courtois, C. A., & Ford, J. D. (2009). *Treating complex traumatic stress disorders: An evidence-based guide.* New York: Guilford Press.

Cryder, C. H., Kilmer, R. P., Tedeschi, R. G., & Calhoun, L. G. (2006). An exploratory study of post-traumatic growth in children following a natural disaster. *American Journal of Orthopsychiatry, 26*(1), 65–69.

Felitti, V. J., Anda, R. F., Nordenberg, D., Williamson, D. F., Spitz, A. M., Edwards, V., ... Marks, J. S. (1998). Relationship of childhood abuse and household dysfunction to many of the leading causes of death in adults. *American Journal of Preventive Medicine, 14*(4), 245–258.

Fergusson, D., Horwood, J., & Lynskey, M. (1996). Childhood sexual abuse and psychiatric disorder in young adulthood, II: Psychiatric outcomes of childhood sexual abuse. *Journal of the American Academy of Child & Adolescent Psychiatry, 35,* 1365–1374.

Finkelhor, D., Turner, H. A., Hamby, S., & Ormrod, R. (2011). *Polyvictimization: Children's exposure to multiple types of violence, crime, and abuse.* Washington, DC: U.S. Department of Justice.

Finkelhor, D., Turner, H. A., Shattuck, A., & Hamby, S. L. (2013). Violence, crime, and abuse exposure in a national sample of children and youth: An update. *JAMA Pediatrics, 167*(7), 614–621.

Flannery, D., Singer, M., & Wester, K. (2001). Violence exposure, psychological trauma, and suicide risk in a community sample of dangerously violent adolescents. *Journal of the American Academy of Child and Adolescent Psychiatry, 40*(4), 435–442.

Foa, E. B., & Hearst-Ikeda, D. (1996). Emotional dissociation in response to trauma. In L. K. Michelson & W. J. Ray (Eds.), *Handbook of dissociation* (pp. 207–244). Boston, MA: Springer.

Froh, J. J., Kashdan, T. B., Yurkewicz, C., Fan, J., Allen, J., & Glowacki, J. (2010). The benefits of passion and absorption in activities: Engaged living in adolescents and its role in psychological well-being. *The Journal of Positive Psychology, 5*(4), 311–332.

Gentzler, A. L., Morey, J. N., Palmer, C. A., & Chit, Y. Y. (2013). Young adolescents' responses to positive events. *The Journal of Early Adolescence, 33,* 1–21.

Gibson, L. E., & Crenshaw, T. (2015). *Self-harm: Trauma and research findings.* Washington, DC: U.S. Department of Veteran's Affairs National Center for PTSD.

Grinhauz, A. S., & Castro Solano, A. (2014). A review of school intervention programs based on character strengths. *Acta Psiquiátrica y Psicológica de América Latina, 60*(2), 121–129.

Halpern, C., Oslak, S., Young, M., Martin, S., & Kupper, L. (2001). Partner violence among adolescents in opposite-sex romantic relationships: Findings from the National Longitudinal Study of Adolescent Health. *American Journal of Public Health, 91*(10), 1679–1685.

Institute of Medicine (IM) and National Research Council (NRC) Committee on the Science of Adolescence. (2011). *The science of adolescent risk-taking: Workshop report.* Washington, DC: National Academies Press.

Janoff-Bulman, R. (1992). *Shattered assumptions: Towards a new psychology of trauma.* New York: Free Press.

Kann, L., McManus, T., Harris, W. A., Shanklin, S. L., Flint, K. H., Hawkins, J., ... Zara, S. (2015). Youth Risk Behavior Surveillance – United States, 2015. *Morbidity and Mortality Weekly Report Surveillance Summaries, 65*(6), 1–18.

Kilpatrick, D. G., Acierno, R., Saunders, B., Resnick, H. S., Best, C. L., & Schnurr, P. P. (2000). Risk factors for adolescent substance abuse and dependence: Data from a national sample. *Journal of Consulting and Clinical Psychology, 68,* 19–30.

Knapp, K. C., & Robinson, J. (2017, March). *Post-traumatic growth: A treatment approach for teen survivors of childhood trauma.* Presentation at the National Youth-At-Risk Conference, Savannah, GA.

Lyons, M. D., Otis, K. L., Huebner, E. S., & Hills, K. J. (2014). Life satisfaction and maladaptive behaviors in early adolescence. *School Psychology Quarterly, 29,* 553–566.

Matulis, S., Resick, P. A., Rosner, R., & Steil, R. (2014). Developmentally adapted cognitive processing therapy for adolescents suffering from post-traumatic stress disorder after childhood sexual or physical abuse: A pilot study. *Clinical Child and Family Psychology Review, 17*(2), 173–190.

McLean, S. (2016). The effect of trauma on the brain development of children. Evidence-based principles for supporting the recovery of children in care. *Australian Institute of Family Studies.* Retrieved from: https://aifs.gov.au/cfca/publications/effect-trauma-brain-development-children.

Meiser-Stedman, R., Smith, P., McKinnon, A., Dixon, C., Trickey, D., Ehlers, A., ... Dalgleish, T. (2017). Cognitive therapy as an early treatment for post-traumatic stress disorder in children and adolescents: A randomized controlled trial addressing preliminary efficacy and mechanisms of action. *Journal of Child Psychology and Psychiatry, 58*(5), 623–633.

Metzl, E. S. (2009). The role of creative thinking in resilience after Hurricane Katrina. *Psychology of Aesthetics, Creativity, and the Arts, 3*(2), 112–123.

Muehlenkamp, J. J., Claes, L., Havertape, L., & Plener, P. (2012). International prevalence of adolescent non-suicidal self-injury and deliberate self-harm. *Child and Adolescent Psychiatry and Mental Health, 6*(10), 1–9.

National Association of State Mental Health Program Directors (NASMHPD) and National Technical Assistance Center for State Mental Health Planning (NTAC). (2004). *The damaging consequences of violence and trauma: Facts, discussion points, and recommendations for the behavioral health system.* Washington, DC: U.S. Department of Health and Human Services (HHS).

National Child Traumatic Stress Network (NCTSN). (2008). *Making the connection: Understanding the link between adolescent trauma and substance abuse.* Retrieved from: https://www.nctsn.org/sites/default/files/resources//understanding_the_links_between_adolescent_trauma_and_substance_abuse.pdf.

National Child Traumatic Stress Network (NCTSN). (2012). *Core curriculum on childhood trauma. The 12 core concepts: Concepts for understanding traumatic stress responses in children and families.* Los Angeles, CA, and Durham, NC: UCLA-Duke University National Center for Child Traumatic Stress.

Office for Victims of Crime (OVC). (2015). *2015 National Crime Victims' Rights Week Resource Guide: Engaging communities, empowering victims.* Washington, DC: U.S. Department of Justice.

Perry, B. D., Pollard, R. A., Blakley, T. L., Baker, W. L., & Vigilante, D. (1995). Childhood trauma, the neurobiology of adaptation, and "use-dependent" development of the brain: How "states" become "traits." *Infant Mental Health Journal, 16,* 271–291.

Reyes, H. L. M., Foshee, V. A., Niolon, P. H., Reidy, D. E., & Hall, J. E. (2016). Gender role attitudes and male adolescent dating violence perpetration: Normative beliefs as moderators. *Health Behavior, 45*(2), 350–360.

Salzinger, S., Rosario, M., Feldman, R., & Ng-Mak, D. (2007). Adolescent suicidal behavior: Associations with preadolescent physical abuse and selected risk and protective factors. *Journal of the American Academy of Child & Adolescent Psychiatry, 46*(7), 859–866.

Seligman, M. E. P. (2002). *Authentic happiness: Using the new positive psychology to realize your potential for lasting fulfillment.* New York: Free Press.

Seligman, M. E. P., Steen, T. A., Park, N., & Peterson, C. (2005). Positive psychology progress: Empirical validation of interventions. *American Psychologist, 60*(5), 410–421.

Seligman, M. E. P., Ernst, R., Gillham, J., Reivich, K., & Linkin, M. (2009). Positive education: Positive psychology and classroom interventions. *Oxford Review of Education, 35,* 293– 311.

Shain, B. (2016). Suicide and suicide attempts in adolescents. *Pediatrics, 138*(1), e20161420.

Spinazzola, J. (2010, April). *Core components in complex trauma intervention.* Presentation at the Complex Trauma Treatment Network Northeast Region Systems of Care Conference, Springfield, MA.

Substance Abuse and Mental Health Services Administration (SAMHSA). (2014). *SAMHSA's concept of trauma and guidance for a trauma-informed approach.* HHS Publication No. (SMA) 14-4884. Rockville, MD: Substance Abuse and Mental Health Services Administration.

Tamannaeifar, M. R., & Motaghedifard, M. (2014). Subjective well-being and its sub-scales among students: The study of role of creativity and self-efficacy. *Thinking Skills and Creativity, 12,* 37–42.

Tedeschi, R. G., & Calhoun, L. G. (1996). The Post-traumatic Growth Inventory: Measuring the positive legacy of trauma. *Journal of Traumatic Stress, 9,* 455–471.

Thompson, R., Lewis, T., Neilson, E. C., English, D. J., Litrownik, A. J., Margolis, B., ... Dubowitz, H. (2017). Child maltreatment and risky sexual behavior: Indirect effects through trauma symptoms and substance use. *Child Maltreatment, 22*(1), 69–78.

Waters, L. (2011). A review of school-based positive psychology interventions. *The Australian Educational and Developmental Psychologist, 28,* 75–90.

RELEVANT LINKS

Association for Behavioral and Cognitive Therapies:

      http://www.abct.org

Australian Institute of Family Studies:

      https://aifs.gov.au

      https://aifs.gov.au/cfca/publications/effect-trauma-brain-development-children

Dating Matters:

      https://vetoviolence.cdc.gov/apps/datingmatters/

The National Child Traumatic Stress Network:

      https://www.nctsn.orgw